Your Life,
Your Purpose,
Your Path

For I Know the Plans
I Have for You

Dan Boozan

Dedication

In this endeavor, I was blessed by the following individuals the Lord placed at critical junctions in my life.

To my wife, Shelly, for her understanding and support as I wrote this book. She has truly been a blessing to me. With all my love, I dedicate this book to her.

To my sister, Robin, whose love, warmth, resolve, and humor in the face of cancer inspires me and will continue to do so until I take my final breath.

To my little sister, Aimee, whose love, joy, and happiness that she brought into my life at an early critical junction meant everything and still does to this day.

To my mother, Alice, for a lifetime of love and instilling in me a deep love of books.

I also dedicate it to my dear friend, an exceptional pastor, and the finest example of Christianity as a way of life that I have ever met, Dan Hatfield. His support at critical junctions in my life, his lucid explanations of our faith, and his comradery did indeed change the trajectory of my life so that this book became possible.

I also wish to dedicate it to a wonderful pastor, Mike Coglan, whose sermons never fail to inspire, instruct, and enlighten me. His explanations of Biblical principles are amazing and ring true in everyday life. Truly his sermons should be required reading for all who study for the pulpit.

I was indeed blessed by the Holy Spirit by having these people in my life.

Table of Contents

Reach Out to the Author and Fellow Christians on Your Path

Email your author at yourlifeyourpurposeyourpath@gmail.com

Facebook: https://www.facebook.com/yourlifeyourpurposeyourpath/

Twitter: @LifePurposePath

Author's Amazon site: www.amazon.com/author/danboozan

Introduction

Your Life, Your Purpose, Your Path is a Biblically inspired journey of self-discovery into your God-decreed purpose and path in life. Christianity is recognized as not just a set of God-decreed beliefs, but as a dynamic way of life constructed upon these beliefs.

We begin with one of the most beloved Biblical passages, Jeremiah 29:11, "'For I know the plans I have for you,' declares the Lord, 'plans to prosper you and not to harm you, plans to give you hope and a future.'" To which we reply, "Okay, what are they?"

This book is a means to answer that question and help you understand God's unique path of hope and a future for you. It is intended to serve as a guide, especially for those uncertain of their future, on how to find that specific life path God is beckoning you down. We will see that Christianity is not only a set of God-given truths but is an active, powerful way of life based on these truths as we follow His path.

You will find that you did indeed come with a user's manual consisting of the passions, inspirations, and desires placed into your heart by the Holy Spirit. Your innate abilities, interests, strengths, and weaknesses will be explored, and your unique mosaic of emotions, talents, and qualities will be studied as your understanding of God's loving plan for you comes alive. The Lord set you apart to be a steward of your rich montage of gifts, and you will learn their meanings and purposes.

Chapters include studies and user exercises regarding notable events that changed the trajectory of your life, what your education actually taught you, how you handle money, books with special meanings to you, a review of work challenges, and a better understanding of marriage issues. You will see what family matters matter, learn from friendships, note the social groups you adhere to, and recognize the teachers who touched you. The importance of physical and emotional well-being, internet sites you go to, use of cell phones, TV shows you love, movies you replay, dreams, prayers with special meanings, and the virtues and vices inherent in your persona will become known. You will even learn from the opposition you will face by the world and satan in discovering the life, purpose, and path intended for you. At the conclusion of each chapter are questions that create "puzzle pieces" of your life.

The gestalt that is you is uncovered and discovered. The jigsaw puzzle pieces of your life are assembled at the conclusion with your life defined, a mission statement created, and a plan of action set for your future.

1. For I Know the Plans I Have for You

One of the most beloved and quoted Biblical passages, Jeremiah 29:11, tells us, "'For I know the plans I have for you,' declares the Lord, 'plans to prosper you and not to harm you, plans to give you hope and a future.'"

Okay, what are they?

That the Lord has specific plans for each of us is undeniable. We only have to commit ourselves to Him to claim them. Proverbs 16: 3-4 enriches us, "Commit to the Lord whatever you do, and He will establish your plans. The Lord works out everything to its proper end."

Central tenants of our lives must be that they have a purpose and a path that can be explored and understood. To do so, we must study and learn from the different facets of our innate core and our interactions with the world – the stuff God put into us and put into our lives. Our interests, abilities, weaknesses, social groups we adhere to, TV shows we are drawn toward, events that changed the trajectory of our lives, friendships, how we handle finances, movies we watch time and again, websites we bring up weekly, books we love, music that speaks to us, etc., can all be critical to God's plan for our lives. These and much more are fodder for this book and your understanding of your life. This gestalt makes up the unique person we are and whom God created and dearly loves. Through careful study of our lives and history, and with His guidance, our lives' purposes and future paths can be unearthed and claimed.

We were born with a personality and many qualities that define our daily lives. Our family and friends influence us. School and work dominate many hours. Media chatters incessantly in many of our lives. Our church lives are hopefully active. Dreams and daydreams can be factors.

Unexpected experiences, serendipitous and otherwise, occur in our lives. The white noise of life is both ceaseless and important. All are vital to understanding ourselves and our future.

We were created in the likeness of God the all-powerful. His destiny for us is the prosperity, hope, and future promised in Jeremiah. We have the God-bestowed ability to make ourselves strong spiritually, as well as physically and mentally. We can appropriate what makes us stronger, yet often we grasp what weakens us. We make ourselves weak, or we make ourselves strong. Regardless, the amount of work is the same.

C.S. Lewis, the great Christian writer, detailed the time he realized that Jesus was the Son of God. It was not a great emotional moment, but just the opposite. He likened it to a man lying in bed asleep, suddenly realizing he was awake.

And awake we must become to the avalanche of guideposts and directions we are given from the Lord for the path he has traced out for us.

However, often these guideposts are glossed over as we busily rush through our day. They are hijacked in our minds by the distractions of the world. Worst of all, satan is determined to subvert the self-discovery of our lives and paths. The devil is not a fool; he will sabotage our way to finding the serenity, happiness, warmth, and joy that has been promised on our predestined path through life.

In this book, we will begin our path of self-discovery by noting the innate talents, interests, weaknesses, idiosyncrasies, and foibles that have shaped us and, in part, led us to our current life position. Later, our experiences, the odd twists in our life histories, and coincidences that have occurred to us will be studied as factors in our present life path. We may find ourselves quite content in our circumstances, or, as Henry David Thoreau wrote, we may lead lives of quiet desperation.

Such a quiet desperation or confusion on how to live life seems to stem from our inability to find the "true north" path we are meant to take of our Lord's specific plans for us.

So, what is our personal "true north" path? How can we determine the life we have been entrusted to live? What can empower us to our promised lives of hope and a future? The answers lie inside our very core and our battles with the world. Our past, current situation, and the promises of our future will all be explored and understood by His grace. Our journey begins now.

Hope and a Future

"'For I know the plans I have for you,' declares the Lord, 'plans to prosper you and not to harm you, plans to give you hope and a future.'"

This passage appears in the middle of Jeremiah, one of the most depressing books of the Bible. The Lord is enraged over His people's doings and will soon send destruction upon them. They will be exiled to a hostile land. Their leader will see his sons killed and then be blinded.

A statistically significant bummer.

Yet in the middle of this distressing book, God's people are told they are to build houses and settle down, marry and give in marriage, to increase in number, and that there will be hope and a future. Despite His great rage, He still acted out of His greater love for them.

Distressing times occur in today's world as well as testified to by the nightly news. Yet we, as Christians, are promised hope and a future.

The Chinese have a wonderful curse, "May you live in interesting times," and without question, we do. They knew what historians call interesting times were absolutely miserable for those going through them. Wars, civil strife, and refugee problems suffice to make our century an interesting time. Jeremiah knew the exact same issues in his era.

I have often said that I am a pessimist about tomorrow, yet an optimist about the day after tomorrow. I remember seeing newsreels from 1950's moralists who decried what that tomorrow was going to be - bobby sox, knee-length skirts, and sock hops. Those were certain to be the moral decay of America.

Now that we have reached the day after that tomorrow, I'm optimistic that bobby sox have not caused the predicted moral destruction of America.

In the era of Jeremiah, God provided His people with hope and a future in the midst of their being exiled. In our era, we can be optimistic that God has given us hope and a future in the midst of the daily news. We should be optimistic that we can realize our hope and a future, seize them, and begin living them.

Stewardship

We can start by scrutinizing the stuff we seem to be made of. As we come into awareness of our gifts and abilities, we better understand 1 Peter 4:9, "Each of you should use whatever gift you have received to serve others, as faithful stewards of God's grace in its various forms." A key foundation of our life's path is our stewardship of the gifts bestowed upon us by the Holy Spirit.

Today, upon hearing the word "steward," we immediately grasp our wallets and prepare for the worst. Yet the word steward actually proclaims you as serving as a guardian of the riches, abilities, interests, and strengths conferred upon you by the Holy Spirit. Stewardship, when the King James Version of the Bible was written, was prestigious. You had been entrusted by the aristocracy to oversee their land and daily business affairs. Your word, on their behalf, was to be carried out as you used your best judgment on finances, personnel, and the health of your domain. You were delegated with great wealth, and that is your position in life today. You are the guardian of the many resources, abilities, and gifts embedded within you.

Among your gifts are your personality traits, work skills, education, dreams, financial acumen, social skills, and more. In seeking and understanding them, God's selected path of the hope and prosperity promised you will become more apparent. God rewards those who earnestly seek Him and will grant them greater self-knowledge of His path for them.

From Adam through today, we are called upon to be guardians of our lives, work, money, time, family, friends, and souls. Further, our society needs us to be stewards of our churches, schools, political systems, social groups we belong to, our neighborhoods, keeping the law, mentoring young people, and much more.

God planned out the talents and abilities He has given us and watches closely how well we use them. To those whom much is given, much is expected. Regardless of our allotment, we are required to use our gifts, not use them for regifting.

We have been charged as stewards of a life, abilities, and strengths. We have been given free will, opportunities, and a future. But what do we choose to do with these? Often the results are mixed at best. We may

16

serve Him well with these, but often we are tripped up by the entanglements of the world like seed growing and being choked by thorn bushes.

One very common, and regrettable, path many walk down is living lives based on comparing themselves to others. We wonder how we are doing financially compared to our neighbors. Our minds are preoccupied asking what our coworkers think of us. We obsess that we might not be as good as our father-in-law. In doing so, we can waste our gifts in a life based on these comparisons. What is worse, these comparisons are often fatally flawed in that we commonly compare our insides to others' outsides. We see our neighbors with their manicured lawns, more money, great looks, and beautiful spouses and feel inferior. How can we possibly measure up? We know how weak, frail, and indecisive we are inside — a bundle of nerves at times and lacking the nerve at others.

Ecclesiastes 4:4 grants us the wisdom we need, "And I saw that all toil and all achievement spring from one person's envy of another. This too is meaningless, a chasing after the wind."

Still, at other times, we judge others by what they lack in comparison to us. That family our church is helping needs to help itself. My subordinates clearly lack ambition. I accomplished more than they ever did by the time I was thirty, and I've left them in the dust ever since. The idea of stewardship of His gifts can be lost inside a straightjacket of pride and arrogance.

Proverbs 8:13 clearly addresses this path, "To fear the Lord is to hate evil; I hate pride and arrogance, evil behavior and perverse speech."

Instead, we must concentrate on serving God as good stewards of the unique life and set of abilities God granted us. In doing so, He will see that our steps are in accordance with His course for us despite our frailty, doubts, and fears. Proverbs 16:9 says, "In their hearts, humans plan their course, but the Lord establishes their steps."

Stewardship will take many forms, including those we may not recognize. I knew a couple whose child was born with the genetic disorder trisomy 13 — a death sentence. Through extraordinary care, love, and grace, the child lived one and a half years and died on a Christmas morning. The purpose of that child's life we can only speculate on, but the impact on their family was unmistakable. They learned a total and uncontested love for a child they would soon bury. They were stewards of the child's life, of love, of sadness, of joy, of serenity, and of the thousands of mixed feelings, duties, and roles they knew in that year and a half. Their stewardship of their abilities, duties, obligations, judgments, emotional chemistry, endurance, and all that was within them were pushed to exhaustion as they served God during this time.

We will be given thousands of lessons and opportunities in our lives, and we must serve as stewards of them for the Lord.

Our Life Puzzle

One truism people, possibly as far back as Adam, seem to feel is that life is a confusing puzzle. And knowing God's plans for us in this quagmire called life is even more baffling.

How can we know His plans for us? Proverbs 20:24 tells us, "A person's steps are directed by the Lord. How then can anyone understand their own way?" His way for us often seems like a jigsaw puzzle without the picture on the front of the box. We feel clueless as to how it will eventually end up looking.

And that jigsaw puzzle of thousands of pieces without the box's picture is our Life Puzzle. It has puzzle pieces of our talents, weaknesses, interests, hates, family interactions, religion, work, schooling, friendships, favorite movies, social groups, health, and the daily grind of just living one day at a time.

As we study ourselves and our lives, we can start to put pieces together. As we put puzzle pieces together, we can begin to glimpse His path for us. Although this will often be a haze, we will be better able to follow the life path He beckons us down.

As you begin to walk this life path, you will start to understand that Christianity is a way of life. Yes, Christianity is based on God's holy words in the Bible, all beliefs based upon that sacred book, and acceptance of His Son as our savior.

But Christianity is not just a noun; it is equally a verb. It is action, an energy, a dynamism, an intensity, a strength, a vitality, a drive, a passion, and ten-thousand things more. Nowhere is this better said than in James 2:17 where we are told, "In the same way, faith by itself, if it is not accompanied by action, is dead." This is the road less traveled, and it is His intended path that you are steward of.

Putting pieces of our Life Puzzle together can show us parts of our probable life path. From there, we can begin an energetic life along that path. That is His hope for us. In living that energetic life along His path for us, we begin to live Christianity as our way of life.

Our progression can be seen as:

- We can begin by starting to put our Life Puzzle pieces together.
- We can then glimpse a picture of God's probable desired life path for us from the assembled pieces.
- We can then begin walking that life path.
- We can then find that walking HIs life path for us is living Christianity as a way of life.

This book is designed to help you piece together your Life Puzzle, see His path for you, and claim the prosperity, hope, and a future He wants for you.

Just as the outside edges of a jigsaw puzzle can indicate what the full picture could be, your future may be indicated within the framework of your past, what constitutes you today, and the many puzzle pieces to be found in your life.

In the next chapter, we will find that innate personality traits, passions, interests, abilities, and weaknesses will be our first set of puzzle pieces. These form the outside edge of your Life Puzzle and give structure to the inner parts.

Additional chapters will cover notable experiences that shaped you, key people placed in your life, work, education, and family members. These puzzle pieces may suggest God's path for your future. How you handle money, websites you frequent, friendships made, music that attracts you, movies you love, TV show you gravitate toward, dreams, health issues, and many more facets of daily life may provide more puzzle pieces and will be studied.

As we learn more, the more we will be able to live Christianity as a way of life. We must follow a pathway of His making, not ours, and in doing so, we will be filling in pieces of our Life Puzzle. It will often not make sense to us, but it will to Him.

My favorite Christian author, C.S. Lewis, enrichens us with his quote, "Fine feelings, new insights, greater interest in 'religion' mean nothing unless they make our actual behavior better." As noted, Christianity is a verb and an action verb at that.

Throughout this book, you will be given "puzzle pieces" tasks. As you work through them, do not worry about doing every task perfectly. Only one person was ever perfect, and they crucified Him because of that. Do expect to do this over time and to spend time reflecting on your childhood.

We will uncover puzzle pieces with each chapter of this book, then assemble them into the picture of what we are and what our future may promise at the end of this book.

To begin this trek, we only need to say, "Thy will be done." In doing so, we have put our first two pieces together. In discovering His will, we must be open to His influences, observe what He gave us, and be intellectually keen in putting our Life Puzzle pieces together.

Pieces we might find could be:

- Personality traits of introversion, optimism, or competitiveness
- A talent for coordinating efforts with others, cooking, or computer programming
- Interests in religion, teaching, or forestry
- Notable weakness with memory, using computers, or alcohol
- Innate qualities such as tenacity, curiosity, and seeking adventure

Then, as we progress in this book, we will look at outside influences in our lives. These puzzle pieces will fill in the middle of the puzzle and show areas of what our path has been and what it might become. In most of our lives, there have been puzzle pieces of people, coincidences, and external actions that have had a decisive impact on our lives and sent our life's trajectory down a different path than we could have expected. Examples could be:

- Being born into an impoverished family, a middle-class family, or a well-to-do family
- Time spent with people who impacted our perceptions of things and encouraged us to follow different paths
- A coincidence that led to a job, meeting our future spouse, or a tragedy in our family

- A strange twist at work or school that led to an opportunity, a new skill, or a notable failure

You will find many empty areas in your Life Puzzle. These are paths you are still to journey down. What you can make out of the surrounding pieces suggests possibilities, but God grants you the freedom to choose what you will follow. God sketched you out before birth in pencil, not in ink. As your life continues, puzzle pieces will be filled in, and you will be able to see God's grander scheme for your life. You will continue to fill in pieces until death.

To each, it will be personal. To each, it will belong to God. As our puzzle is filled in, we will start to understand better what He intended for us. In a final retrospective of our lives, we may not know God's meanings for large parts of our Life Puzzle, but they will be necessary to Him. When we finally shed this mortal coil and meet Him, we will finally know His entire plan for us and its meaning. We will see the completed puzzle as we are received by God. For some, they will hear the words, "Well done, good and faithful servant!"

Where Will Our Path Lead?

Where does our Life Path lead? Where are we going? We are going to God. He made us for no other purpose. Our path will seem convoluted with many sub-paths, detours, tunnels, and bridges along the way. It will often make no sense, yet He designed it to serve Him and eventually lead us to Him if we follow.

Intertwining shorter paths will make up the longer, straighter path we are to tread. We are allowed to use our will to bypass His will, straighten our path to Him, detour us far away, jump closer to Him, or even send us into oblivion. How we use our self-will will be a major determinant of how successful we are on our life's trek to Him.

We must try to follow His direction as a matter of honoring Him, knowing that He blesses obedience. In 1 Samuel 2:30, we are told, "Those who honor me, I will honor." God blesses and honors those who trust and obey Him.

God has set in motion the laws of nature to govern our planet, He allowed His Son to die in our place, and He sent us the Holy Spirit. He has given us much, and He has given us free will. We are allowed to change our personal lives and to change history. But regardless of the changes we make and upheavals we experience, He will be our stability. He gives us free rein over much of our lives, but, almost imperceptibly, we will find a steady stream of love coming from Him into our lives, especially as we wander off our path. Unceasingly, He will beckon us back onto our trail to Him.

Our path, most assuredly, will hold disease, pride, anger, pain, hardship, and oppression, yet He will see to it that we have small mercies placed on our path. He loves us so much that He cannot bear not to try to reassure us. We must listen for the sound of His love. It is there and maybe loudest when we are at our lowest.

Our goal is reunification with God with our coming back as prodigal sons and daughters. Jeremiah 1:5 starts, "Before I formed you in the womb, I knew you, before you were born, I set you apart." He set Jeremiah apart as a prophet. He sets each of us apart specifically to be ourselves. Our purpose in life is to follow our path to God using the life He has provided us with and our free will.

Trying

Nothing may be more important than a willingness to try. God wants us to try to understand and follow His path and purposes for us. This may be especially so when we are at our lowest.

We remember in the twenty-first chapter of John, that the apostles' leader, Peter, denied Jesus three times just before His crucifixion. Peter's stock within the group must have dropped to less than nothing. He probably had as much self-esteem as a peeled zero.

Only days later, undoubtedly numb from the shock of having his Lord crucified, Peter was found fishing. It may well have been that Peter was resigning himself back to the obscurity of his previous life.

Then, on the shore, the risen Christ asked him if he loved Him using the term "agape," the highest form of love. Peter replied using the "phileo" version of love, which is brotherly love. He meant he would try, but felt unable to offer "agape." He no doubt felt the sting of his denials and felt unworthy of promising he would love at the highest level. Again, Jesus asked if he loved Him using the term "agape." Again, Peter replied using "phileo." For a third time, Jesus asked, but used the word "phileo" and Peter replied using "phileo," again indicating he would try. That was what Jesus wanted to hear. The three denials were wiped clean by three answers that he would try. That is what God wants from us, a desire to try.

Jesus ordained that the Christian church was to be built upon a rock named Peter, but what kind of rock is that? A soft one at times, but resilient at others, judging by Peter's three denials followed by his three affirmations. He was a common man, like common coal, who, under pressure at the end, turned from coal into a diamond. Supposedly his last request was to be crucified upside down because he felt unworthy to be crucified as His Lord was. Stoking the fire of this coal, we uncover the heat that started our early church. Peter's writings and missionary work proclaimed the gospel of Christ in this new world of Christianity, forming the rock foundation that built our church. He simply tried.

As we begin to try to live God's plan for us, as little of it as we might know, things will start to change, and we might even notice them. An attitude of self-seeking may slip away. Impatience may morph into concern for others. Our belief in Him may strengthen. Trusting Him may become more apparent.

Does our belief in Him need to be strong for us to begin our personal mission? Absolutely not. God simply wants the beginning of an effort from us. Mark 9:24 tells us what we must be able to say, "I do believe; help me overcome my unbelief!"

Must we come to Him out of purely altruistic motives? It's not possible. Self-seeking seems to be inherent in our DNA, and we almost instinctively try to find an angle that will benefit us. He knows we will. He created us. That doesn't matter to Him. We simply have to ask for His help in finding our path, regardless of how mixed our motives might be.

Must we wait to come to Him when we are spiritually sound and active in our church? A resounding "No" from heaven is our answer. He absolutely does not want us to wait for anything. One of God's greatest miracles, from our perspective, is that He loves us most when we are our most unlovable. God takes us as what we are and where we are, regardless of how wretched that might be at any moment. Often, we come to Him for no reason other than we are in pain. He knows that and could not care less. All of heaven rejoices that we simply reached out to Him.

Our attitude may be the first thing we notice changing, with the greatest example possibly being Paul. Paul had a complete change in attitude and didn't need an "attitude adjustment" hour at the bar. He had set out to annihilate the infant Christian movement when God took him on His specific path for him. Philippians 4:12-13 shows what his attitude became later in life, "I know what it is to be in need, and I know what it is to have plenty. I have learned the secret of being content in any and every situation, whether well fed or hungry, whether living in plenty or in want. I can do all this through Him who gives me strength." Paul had mastered controlling his attitude through the grace of the Holy Spirit. He was content in his circumstances, complacent in his needs, yet a firebrand of ambition in spreading the gospel.

We may not notice how we are changing, but others will notice it. Proverbs 27:19 tells us, "As water reflects the face, so one's life reflects the heart. "As our heart changes, so will our lives, as we begin walking His path.

As we discover His path for us, we also may think that it changes, in our myopic eyes, as we walk down it. The military says that the first casualty of war is the plan. We need to be nimble, flexible, and to trust and obey our God. His plan is rarely a straight line in our feeble eyesight. Understanding this is required to discover our path.

We will find that the Lord often works by preparing things for us far in advance, which may include the classes we take, passages of books we read, and chance encounters with people. Their impact may be intended for many years later. The Lord, to our way of thinking, leads us in mysterious ways, but lead us He will.

What we see in our lives and how we see our lives will change as we try to live Christianity, not only as a set of beliefs, but as a way of life. We will view our life differently than we viewed it ten years, five years, or even a year ago. We will see things from a new perspective and act in a markedly different manner by actively and deliberately living Christianity. Our vision of our lives and our future will be clear. C.S. Lewis put it well, "I believe in Christianity as I believe that the sun has risen: not only because I see it, but because by it I see everything else."

Starting

How much of His life path for us do we need to know to start living Christianity as our way of life? Very little.

Look at the size of the DNA of a mustard seed. It is almost nonexistent, yet it determines the growth of a majestic tree and its lifecycle. It dictates how the tree responds to changes in its environment, how it reacts to drought and flood, and how its growth accelerates, then declines with age.

Once we have an inkling of the DNA of His path for us, we can proceed, knowing He will put others in our lives, make changes to our circumstances, and bring us joy and heartache, triumphs and trials, sadness and serenity. Today, we can try to understand a tiny sliver of His plans for us, and, in doing so, we take a single step on the path He beckons us down.

The feeding of the five thousand in John 6:1-13 was not just an exercise in the culinary arts, but a statement that a small amount can be immensely magnified when God works on it. And work on us He will, regardless of how little knowledge of His plan we may start with. We must trust the truism that with God, all things are possible.

We are to focus on God's direction for us, regardless of what we call obstacles. If we have a small talent (aka a puzzle piece), He may magnify it. Moses thought he had no oratory ability and told God to give the leadership of His people to Aaron. The Lord took Moses' minuscule leadership and speaking abilities and magnified them so that he could lead a great nation. Moses, like us, had his path to follow, and the Lord worked through him as was necessary to achieve His goals.

When do we need to know His path for us to claim the life we are meant to lead and the rewards inherent in it? Our youth? By college? In our thirties? Certainly, by forty?

A Biblical story is instructive. Matthew 20:1-16 tells us the parable of workers hired at different times in the day, yet they all were paid the same. Those hired at the beginning of the day thought their pay should have been greater than those hired toward the end, but that is not how God works.

God will reward those who are saved at the "end of the day," that is late in life, as well as those who are saved and lead lives according to His

Word from their youth, or the "beginning of the day." The last selected are "in the market" or living worldly, non-Christian lives, while those selected early in the day work harder throughout their lives or the "heat of the day." Regardless of when we begin, all can walk the path God has planned for us. Our rewards will be the same in heaven, but our timings different on earth.

We start by trying to understand what the Lord wants for us and from us and then set our earthly plans accordingly, knowing that it is His purpose that must triumph. Proverbs 19:21 informs us, "Many are the plans in a person's heart, but it is the Lord's purpose that prevails." In a supreme example, Paul had in his plans the elimination of Christianity but ended up writing much of the New Testament.

It is not important how we start or when. It is important that we start.

And now, we will start.

2. Personality Traits, Interests, Abilities, and Weaknesses

Now, ground zero, a look at your total personal package. The hand you were dealt by the Lord. You will explore the unique attributes that make you that indispensable person God dearly loves. He set you apart, gave you a one-of-a-kind blend of traits, talents, and abilities and wants you to live Christianity as your way of life. His Son's life is your ideal, and the Holy Spirit is your escort. You now need to discover what is innately inside of you and use those pieces to assemble the outer frame of your Life Puzzle.

You may not feel you were given the right set of attributes for your life and mission, but you were. One of the most fundamental problems we have when we look at ourselves is that we do so by comparing ourselves to others. More specifically, we compare our inner set of feelings, insecurities, problems, and emotions to the outer shell we see of others. They have that job we would dearly love; they enjoy great looks; money isn't an issue for them; they have leadership abilities, and they have the life we wish we had. Yet it's guaranteed that they have frailties, problems, and underlying fears just as we do.

Even those who seem to have everything going for them can internally feel life going horribly wrong. They may hide it better and put on an aura of invincibility, but they too are burdened. The tragic suicides of Robin Williams, Marilyn Monroe, Kurt Cobain, Ernest Hemingway, Freddie Prinze, and so many more are instructive.

The paths of others are different than the one set down for you, but they are still paths with concerns and conquests as yours will be.

Regardless of what we think we are and what we have, we have a life, a purpose, a path, and a guide in the Lord.

So how do we discover our personality traits, interests, assets, and liabilities? Through prayer, questioning, and observation. One of the most surprising things you will find is that a talent, skill, strength, or trait you didn't know you had may suddenly appear, and you will find yourself saying, "Where did that come from?" It may be a small sliver of an ability that you must develop, but it was given to you to use and serve the Lord with.

You may find that you are a team player and thrive on committees, group projects, and working groups. Then again, you may find you are a staunch individualist and called to cut your own path through life. You may take to heart the adage, "God so loved the world that He didn't send a committee."

Some interests and abilities may be so entrenched in you that they may be hard to recognize. You may not be able to see the largest tree in the forest when you are sitting in that tree. Here the observations of others can be useful. A trusted friend or family member can be invaluable as a reviewer of your personality trait assessment, provider of a reality check, and may serve as a devil's advocate as needed.

As an example, I was unable to see how tenacious I could be when trying to resolve a problem until it was duly pointed out by a friend. Sometimes I seemed constitutionally incapable of letting go of a problem. I was like a dog who could not give up a bone. I placed that as a personality trait that, at times, has served me well and at others left me with a bare bone and aching teeth.

Still, another personality trait I know I possess is that I have good judgment. Good judgment comes from experience. Experience comes from making bad judgments. Enough said.

Once we have a better picture of our personality traits, interests, abilities, and weaknesses, we can look at how they can impact the rest of our lives and better gauge the foundation God has laid down within us. At the convergence of our personality traits, our interests, our abilities, and our limitations, we find our first guidepost. We reach that first milestone on our quest to find God's predefined journey for our lives. Our Life Puzzle's border will be built.

We will now look at our personality traits, then interests, then abilities and weaknesses in turn. Do not think you must do this section perfectly. You are simply trying to find indicators of what God has decreed would make up that complex person called you. Each of us was granted very specific gifts by God as recognized in 1 Corinthians 7:7 where Paul tells us, "I wish that all of you were as I am. But each of you has your own gift from God; one has this gift, another has that." We are now trying to identify these gifts, both the obvious and those just beneath our understanding. We will make a good faith effort and leave the results in God's hands.

Personality Traits

Our personality traits may stem from our biological settings, as well as child-rearing and interactions with others. Together they help define our personality the way it is at this moment. It has been theorized that a child's personality is largely formed by the age of seven (Johnson, 2010), with some claiming much of it is determined by the age of three. (Avshalom Caspi, Children's Behavioral Styles at Age 3 are Linked to their Adult personality traits at age 26, 2003)

It is important to note that these qualities are personified and observable in our early youth and largely do not alter as we live out our decades. They are our personality fingerprints. We simply do not outgrow our fingerprints. They are the stuff we are made of. The extroverts remain outgoing, and the introverts remain as such. There is stability in personality traits that can be measured by daily observation of our lives, actions, and thoughts. The free spirits dance with free reins on their passions, and the geeks dance with pocket protectors on their souls.

One recommended starting place to gauge our personality traits would be to take one of the personality inventory tests that are available. Notable examples are the Myers-Briggs Type Indicator (MBTI) test, Minnesota Multiphasic Personality Inventory (MMPI), Sixteen Personality Factor Questionnaire (16PF), and the Revised NEO Personality Inventory (based on the Five-Factor Model of personality) personality tests. These can be administered at a local college's counseling center, possibly a high school, and, increasingly, online. Your strongest and weakest personality traits and attributes will be uncovered, and perhaps career matches will be provided. Some tests are now free over the internet, e.g. *www.16personalities.com.* You may wish to take several tests to better see the core traits inherent within you.

Depending on the test and results, you may uncover portions of your personality that are buried just below your awareness. Some traits you may be painfully cognizant of, and others may have seemed evident since birth. Being gregarious, generous, or a low-energy person may well describe you or the exact opposite may be found. The point is not whether these are good or bad attributes, but that they are the way you were made. Dan was meant to be Dan, Shelly was meant to be Shelly, and Chelsea was meant to be Chelsea. What is important is to recognize our God-given inventory of traits and start to recognize how they are meant to be used. We are to be good stewards of our lives, and that includes the unique collection of qualities we have been granted. They are the underpinnings on how we are to live our lives, interact with others, and serve our Lord. They will serve as part of the border of our Life Puzzle.

An example of a personality trait you may find is dwelling on the past. Do you tend to say coulda, shoulda, woulda, about things that might have gone differently if you had reacted differently, or do you plunge ahead regardless of the past? A born quarterback will put out of his mind the play that just happened. There is a new situation, and that is all that matters. There is no coulda, shoulda, woulda, but a new situation he must place all of his concentration on.

If you prefer, instead of taking one of the standard tests, you can come up with a customized list of personality traits. You can look through the list of characteristics provided below and select the ones that you seem to exhibit the most, regardless of what you may want to place down for yourself. For example, in the following list of attributes, you may want to mark down being gregarious when around people, yet are rarely that way. That might be how you want to be, but since you seldom act that way, it would be a poor selection. If you are often cautious in approaching new people but dislike that aspect of yourself, it could be a selection because it is one you tend to act upon.

What we do is evidence of what we are. This is especially true when we are caught by surprise or are placed in unexpected situations. Are we upset, angry, understanding, patient, passive, or irritated? For example, if a coworker comes to you just before you are to leave work and says they need to be driven home because their car isn't working, how do you react? These moments can guide our selections. The reaction of a person when they are thrust into an unexpected situation can be the best indicator of the kind of person that they are.

You may also get clues from how you unconsciously act in everyday situations. Are you an aggressive driver who cuts others off? Do you walk noticeably slower than others around you? Do you wolf down your lunch and are impatient to get back to work? Do you find yourself justifying your actions before others when it is not needed? These behaviors may be instilled deeply within you and can reflect facets of your personality.

You may also find that taking personality inventory tests or selecting from the items below is influenced by your current mood. Feeling depressed can skew the results as can feeling on top of the world. Try to be aware of your mood and attempt to select items based on how you normally feel and act.

If you elect to use the following list of personality traits, then select ten to fifteen that you seem to act upon the most or feel the most frequently. These will constitute your strengths. Yes, they may encompass elements you may not see as strengths, such as being intolerant or having anger, yet they are the ones you act on.

Then denote ten to fifteen you never or seldom act upon. These will constitute your weaknesses. Once again, they may encompass qualities you might not see as weaknesses, such as kindness or being adventurous, but you simply do not act on these.

You want to develop a picture of the personality traits God had ingrained into you and those you were not given. Let how you typically act guide you.

The list below is by no means comprehensive, so feel free to add any additional traits you feel pertinent to your own distinct case.

After taking a test(s) and/or using the list below, go to the traits you most frequently act on (your strengths list) and write down two examples of how you have exhibited each. If you cannot come up with two ways you have demonstrated such a trait sometime in your life, then possibly it is a weak quality that should not be on the list.

Next, note the traits you listed as weaknesses or that a test(s) indicates you rarely act upon and learn from them. Your path will probably not include these, but you can know yourself better by understanding them and the limits that are being placed upon you by not having them in your personality makeup.

After these efforts, step back and consider why God has bestowed or not bestowed select personality traits upon you. Your strengths are there for a purpose, as are your weaknesses. Reflection on what their purposes could be is what you need at this stage.

Able to set priorities	Competitive
Abrasive	Compulsive
Accepting	Conceited
Adaptable	Confident
Adventurous	Conformist
Aggressive	Conscientious
Agreeable	Conservative
Analytical	Considerate
Anger	Contemplative
Anxious	Conventional
Apathetic	Cooperative
Apologetic	Creative
Appreciative	Critical
Argumentative	Curious
Articulate	Decisive
Artistic	Dedicated
Assertive	Demanding
Bad judgment	Dependent
Benevolent	Detail-oriented
Blunt	Determined
Builder	Difficult
Calculating	Disciplined
Calm	Discouraging
Capable	Disobedient
Caring	Disorganized
Cautious	Dominating
Charismatic	Dramatic
Cheerful	Dutiful
Circumspect	Dwells on the past
Compassion	Early morning person

Easy going

Emotional

Empathetic

Energetic

Envious

Excitable

Faithful

Family peacekeeper

Family therapist

Fatalistic

Fearful

Fickle

Fiery

Flexibility

Focused

Forceful

Forgetful

Forgiving

Frugal

Generous

Gloomy

Good judgment

Greedy

Gregarious

Hardworking

Helpful

Hesitant

High-energy person

High-spirited

Honest

Humble

Humorous

Idealistic

Imaginative

Impatient

Impractical

Impressionable

Impulsive

Inconsiderate

Indecisive

Independent

Individualist

Inhibited

Insightful

Integrity

Intolerant

Irrational

Irresponsible

Kindness

Lazy

Leadership

Logical

Loquacious

Low-energy person

Loyal

Makes friends easily

Mellow

Methodical

Modest

Moody

Narcissistic

Narrow-minded

Negativity

Night person

Noncompetitive

Non-emotional

Non-religious

Obedient

Objective

Opinionated

Optimistic

Organized

Outspoken

Passionate

Dan Boozan

Passive
Patient
Perfectionist
Perseveres
Persuasive
Planner
Playful
Possessive
Practical
Problem solver
Procedure oriented
Procrastinating
Protective
Proud
Punctual
Questioning
Quiet
Rational
Realistic
Regretful
Rejecting
Reliable
Religious
Reserved
Resourceful
Responsible
Restrained
Retiring
Routine oriented
Sarcastic
Scholarly
Scornful
Selfish

Selfless
Self-sufficient
Sensitive
Serious
Shy
Sloppy
Sociable
Solitary
Spontaneous
Stable
Stingy
Strict
Strong-willed
Stubborn
Submissive
Suspicious
Sympathetic
Systematic
Takes initiative
Team player
Tenacious
Thoughtless
Timid
Tolerant
Tough
Trusting
Uncooperative
Understanding
Undisciplined
Unreliable
Vulnerable
Warm
Witty

Common Sense

One commonly overlooked, yet vital, trait that needs to be singled out is common sense. It was given to humans in varying doses it seems and sometimes we run out of it. Occasionally it can be shared by a friend or group. Often it is deliberately sidestepped. It is important and needs to be used and expanded on during our lives.

The more emotional one gets in debates with others, the less one listens to others and their viewpoints, and with any level of alcohol or other drugs, the more our dipstick in our common sense oil pan shows it has burned out our tail pipes.

Common sense is sound practical judgment on everyday matters. It is the basic ability to perceive, understand, and judge the elements in our lives. We act reasonably toward others, including our two-year-old who kept us up all last night. Nearly all people possess enough to function and even thrive in the modern world.

In society, it is seen as the good judgment of average people acting as a group.

The term was popularized at the time of, and was an instigator of, the American revolution. *Common Sense* was the name of the most important pamphlet ever written by an American. Thomas Paine published it in 1776 advocating independence from Great Britain. It championed a radical uprising and fought for egalitarian government. In proportion to the population of the colonies at that time, it had the largest sale and distribution of any book published in American history. Given that the conservatives at that time wished to remain with the king and Britain, it was an incendiary liberal book. The idea of democracy and representative government, instead of a monarchy, was fanatical and revolutionary in that time. Today, because of those extremists, the United States has the oldest democracy in the world. Since that era, the nations of the world have looked to America for guidance, support, and inspiration in building their democracies.

Obviously, the term can be attached to radical movements or we would still be serving the British monarchy. However, for the past two-hundred years common sense has been American society's measuring

35

rod of sensibility, rationality, practicality, and logical thoughts, words, and deeds.

Yet disturbingly, common sense is being used as a banner today for hatred and radicalism by some. In their redefinition of this phrase, sensibility and rationality are branded as a liability, or even a danger, to some social movement leaders.

Common sense is utilized when we see facts and make reasonable conclusions. However, some social movement leaders try, and to varying extents succeed, in twisting facts into what suits their agenda. Many people today find it simpler to be like sheep and let others lead them on what to think. They are told to accept what they are being fed, regardless of reality, and, most importantly, shut up.

What I am referring to was clearly shown when fifty-one Muslims were shot and killed in Christchurch, New Zealand in 2019 by a man who wrote a white supremacist, anti-immigrant manifesto. I was distressed at both the horror of the blood bath and, later, that a noted right-wing commentator championed the idea that the assassin could actually be a radical liberal who wanted to smear the conservative movement.

Left-wing extremists also attempt to lead their followers with unrealities. One example, as of this writing, is their (totally unproven) howls of how President Trump is a Russian finger-puppet on Russian President Putin's little finger.

Common sense will be needed by you on your journey possibly more than any other trait. You will find that the angrier and more enraged social leaders of the world will rarely encourage you to use your common sense. You will be told your position is one of obedience. You are never to question their leadership or consider hearing the other side.

They will hate you when you use common sense to learn and consider other ideas than what you are fed by them. So will satan.

Interests

Similarly, it is recommended that you consider taking a standard interest inventory test. The Strong-Campbell Interest Inventory, Kuder Occupational Interest Survey, and others are available at colleges, high schools, and increasingly over the internet. Some interest inventory tests are even free online. They can help you uncover what truly interests you, what is of minor interest, and the items you have no interest in.

It has been said that if you want to know what your true interests are, look at your interests as a child. What interested you in your early years? What did you read about? What did you dream of building? If you wanted to save the environment, what did you think or plan to do about it? Did you plan things, organize activities, want to be in plays, enjoy puzzles, or what? Did you play with animals, dissect ant colonies, invent games, lived to play sports, or were happiest watching TV?

Today's youth may well answer a resounding "Yes" to playing computer games, watching movies, and fiddling with cell phones, which brings up a question. Should we be concerned about the most recent edition of children and their different interests, behaviors, and actions? Without question – No!

Reportedly in the ruins of ancient Pompeii, one of the inhabitants wrote graffiti stating their concern for the future of their nation when they observed the youth of their day. Plato was quoted as saying "What is happening to our young people? They disrespect their elders; they disobey their parents. They ignore the law. They riot in the streets inflamed with wild notions. Their morals are decaying. What is to become of them?"

Cicero listed his thoughts on his era from bad to worse, "Times are bad. Children no longer obey their parents, and everyone is writing a book." Everyone is writing a book. Even then, Cicero must have known that writing is nature's gift to the ulcer.

What we know of our post-Pompeiian youth is that they, too, have their own interests, wants, and ways of expressing themselves that are as natural as the pre-Pompeiian generations were. Somehow, we have managed to survive their youth and our youth, although I now better understand George Bernard Shaw, who said, "Youth is wasted on the young."

You may well find that your interests change as the world changes. For example, technology changes have been relentless, and society has changed as a result. The technology you saw when you were ten years old may have enthralled you, and when you turned twenty-five that technology was ancient, but a love for that type of technology may have been instilled deeply within you.

37

In the 1980s, microcomputers entered the workplace, and something I never dreamed of touching became playthings I thrived on. They appealed to my analytic side, my problem-solving interests, and my designer side as I wrote programs. Today's society seems powered by these micro beasts. I enthusiastically placed computers as one of my interests.

If you decide to forego using a standard interest inventory test, then you can optionally go through the following list of items. Select ten to fifteen interests that you currently have an interest in or had an interest in when younger, although this time, you do not have to have acted upon them. For example, you may have always had an interest in animals, yet never had the chance to own a pet. You may put that down as an interest since you may well be able to explore it in the future.

When completed, step back and contemplate why God placed these interests in you. He may well have bestowed within you a significant interest for a significant purpose. You may have been entrusted to be a good steward of such an interest.

I found that my interests were for the more solitary pursuits, and that helped me to better gauge my path. You may find your list contains more social activities, intellectual challenges, or outdoor-oriented interests.

Once again, this is not a comprehensive list by any means. Add any interests that you have that are not on this list.

When done, consider if God is guiding you with one or several of these interests. Could they be a beacon you are to follow, or are they only to serve a minor, but pleasant aspect of your life. Keep an open mind as to their possibilities a week, a year, or a decade from now.

Amateur radio	Camping or Hiking
Animals	Clubs/organizations
Arts	Coaching/teaching
Astronomy	Collecting things
Automobiles	Community activities
Bicycling	Computers
Board games/puzzles	Computer games
Boating/sailing	Conversations
Books	Cooking
Building	Dancing

Developing ideas
Dining
Doing things for others
Drama/Theater
Ecology/Recycling
Educational courses
Electronics
Entertaining others
Environment
Farming/Forestry
Fashion/Jewelry
Fishing
Fitness/Health
Flying
Gambling
Gardening
Genealogy
Geocaching
Handling money
Helping others
History
Home decorating
Home improvement
Home repair
Hunting
Indoor games
Intellectual challenges
Internet
Investing
Learning a foreign language
Making models (ships, railroading, etc.)
Managing a business
Managing others
Martial Arts
Math
Mechanical work

Medicine
Movies/Theater
Music
News
Observing nature
Origami
Performing arts
Photography/Making videos
Planning things
Politics
Public speaking/ Storytelling
Puppetry
Reading
Recreational activities
Religious activities
Remote controlled planes/ boats
Researching/studying things
Scientific activities
Scrapbooking
Self-improvement
Selling things
Sewing/household crafts
Shopping
Software design
Spelunking/Climbing
Sports
Starting a business
Storm chasing
Tea/Coffee tastings
Teaching
Technical work
Travel
TV shows
Video games
Volunteer work
Water sports/activities

Wine tasting	Writing
Woodworking	Yoga/meditation
Words	Youth activities
Working with others	
Working with your hands	

Abilities and Weaknesses

Your abilities and weaknesses may be obvious or barely recognizable. Notable weaknesses may be improved upon, and major abilities may atrophy due to lack of use. Our personal biases can present an uneven assessment in that we often hesitate to admit to our weaknesses, while minor abilities can be propelled out of proportion once our ego gets wind of the list to be created. So, there are many possibilities and pitfalls when we attempt to list our abilities and weaknesses.

Towering abilities and obvious weaknesses can be readily identified. Abilities in math, handling money, and home repair may be well known. Weaknesses in tolerating cold weather, a poor driving record, and judgment in choosing friends may need to be acknowledged. For example, I seem unable to master cooking. When asked if I do my cooking from scratch, I typically reply that if you eat my cooking, you will scratch for a week.

Seemingly trivial items can be listed in either camp. You may indicate your handwriting as a weakness and the tonal quality of your voice as an ability. Napoleon's handwriting was so poor that a general mistook a letter from him to be a map. Certain vocal types lend themselves well to authority figures, singers, and actors.

My public speaking ability started as a liability; then, it became an interest, and, after significant practice, became a strength I used in teaching. Sometimes weaknesses follow such a course if God has decreed them to be on your path. In the Bible, we find where God took minor abilities and transformed them into strengths to serve Him. David had an ability with a sling but no background as a warrior, until he met Goliath.

One notable example of something important you could select, as either an ability or weakness, is your memory. You may have a memory as astounding as Harry Lorayne's, author of *The Memory Book*. He would meet three-hundred audience members entering the TV studio, then name each of them during the broadcast.

Then again, we may have a memory as weak as the hapless student-athlete Jerry Lucas spoke of in the same book. When asked his name, the student paused, then answered. Upon being asked once more, he paused still again before stating his name. When asked why he hesitated, the student explained that he had to hear the song "Happy Birthday" in his mind to remind him of his name.

As important as having an analytical mind might be, memory may be a more pertinent ability for most of us. Like an analytical mind, it can also be trained to serve us on our path better.

Memory for facts and figures, memory for names and people, memory for jokes, etc., all should be considered for this ability. In my experience, I would say Austin O'Malley had it right when he said, "Memory is a crazy woman that hoards colored rags and throws away food." I have a good memory for trivia; hence, I tell others I have a trivial mind.

Here, you are to review the following list of abilities and skills and indicate ten to fifteen as strong abilities and ten to fifteen as weaknesses. Once again, add any items you wish to the list. After you have your two listings, reflect on your list of strong abilities and come up with two actual instances where they served as strengths. As before, review your weaknesses and try to understand what God wants you to learn about yourself from them.

Able to see the big picture
Adaptability
Analytical
Brainstorming
Building
Can work alone
Coaching
Collaborating
Communication
Comprehend ideas
Computer skills
Conflict resolution
Cooking
Counseling
Creative thinking
Critical thinking
Customer service
Decision making
Designing
Driving
Editing
Entertaining
Evaluation
Expressing ideas
Financial
Following instructions
Foreign languages
Helpful to others
Imagination
Information gathering
Information management
Inspection
Judgment in friends
Leadership
Listening
Logical thinking

Make friends readily
Management
Math / Statistical
Mechanical
Meeting new people
Memory
Motivating others
Multi-tasking
Musical
Negotiation
Numerical analysis
Operating equipment
Organizing
People skills
Persuasiveness
Physical health
Planning
Precision work
Problem-solving
Public speaking
Reliability
Repairing equipment
Research
Resolving conflicts
Responsibility
Risk-taking
Running meetings
Sales
Studying
Summarizing data
Supervising others
Supportive of others
Taking the initiative
Teaching
Team building
Technical work
Tenacity

Time management	Work with details
Voice quality	Work with ideas
Weather tolerance	Work with your hands
Work under pressure	Work with your mind
Work well with others	Writing

When completed, step back and contemplate why God has provided these. He will look at the abilities He has bestowed upon us and see how well we served as stewards of them. To those whom much is given, much is expected. The Bible tells us of the parable of the servants and the talents. Of the servant He gave five talents to, He expected much. Of the servant He gave one talent to, He expected little, but He still expected him to use his talent. The parable was of money some two-thousand years ago, but He has granted us abilities and weaknesses in our lives today.

Paul tells us in 1 Corinthians 12:4-6, "There are different kinds of gifts, but the same Spirit distributes them. There are different kinds of service, but the same Lord. There are different kinds of working, but in all of them and in everyone it is the same God at work."

So, what should we do after we isolate our strong and week abilities? Should we work on our weaknesses to become better balanced? If we find that we lack a math ability, should we work to make it a strength? Probably not.

By working on weaknesses and neglecting our strengths, we may make our weaknesses less weak, but we are only occasionally able to transform them into strengths. Only infrequently do we have a calling to journey down such a path. Our strengths are what we seem to be called to focus on. These riches were placed in us for a purpose, and we grow best through our strengths. By working with your strengths, you will be able to expand upon them and accelerate their growth. They are blessings that can not only be used to serve the Lord, but when we use them, such as at work, we find that work no longer seems to be a burden, but what we were meant to do all along. Follow your God-given blessings and trust in the Lord.

Puzzle Pieces

Now review and, optionally, share your lists with a trusted friend, spouse, or family member. A reality check can be jarring but necessary. Sometimes a verbal whack on the side of the head loosens and lets things flow as they need to. You may optionally let that trusted person come up with a few personality traits and abilities they clearly see in you. The comparison of your lists with theirs may be an eye-opener. Edit your lists as you feel is needed.

Next, create a brief essay of no more than one page describing yourself based on your lists. Define how you might be able to serve the Lord with your unique talents, blessings, and limitations. Emphasize a few personality traits, interests, abilities, and weaknesses that genuinely stand out. You do not need to cover all of them. Do not be concerned if you have not explored or used these heavily. The time for them may be set by the Lord for the future. Deeply consider why the Lord gave certain ones to you and left you bereft of others.

Now that our lists are made and the essay complete, we have an idea of our gifts from the Holy Spirit and know better how to oversee the life path we have been given. The outline of our Life Puzzle is complete. As 1 Peter 4:10 tells us, "Each of you should use whatever gift you have received to serve others, as faithful stewards of God's grace in its various forms."

Our initial gifts, traits, foibles, interests, abilities, and weaknesses have been revealed. Next, we will look at critical junctions, the impact of others, schooling, work, money, the impact of media, and more.

The Right Stuff

In his mesmerizing book by the same name, Tom Wolfe spoke of those having "the right stuff" for their mission. He gave the example of pilots who were told to have a good breakfast prior to flying. They would be more effective and do better flying if they did so. Instead, they jumped into their planes with nothing but a cup of coffee in their stomachs and did outstanding flying. They had the right stuff, and some bacon and eggs weren't going to make any difference.

You have been given the right stuff for your life by God; you just need to appropriate it and start flying. On your path, you do not go slowly in the fast lane of your abilities, interests, and strengths.

You were put in that lane for a reason.

3. Foundation Puzzle Pieces

We have built our Life Puzzle's outline with what comprises us in traits, interests, abilities, and weaknesses. To firm up this one-piece wide outline of what we will find of ourselves and our lives, we will add a second layer inside our completed framework. These are foundation puzzle pieces. As the word "foundation" implies, they give our outline strength and grant us better knowledge of what we are and who we are to become.

Spiritual Grist for the Mill

Foundation puzzle pieces are spiritual components in our lives that underlie our very essence. They may vary some from person to person but are mostly consistent between us. It seems God intended us to know and live under these spiritual workings of life.

We will find many foundation puzzle pieces during our days under the sun, but you may find that some of the more important ones, the ones affecting our daily lives, seem to be among the following.

- Christianity is not just a set of God-decreed truths but a way of life.
- You are required to serve as the steward of your rich montage of gifts, traits, abilities, and weaknesses. They were deliberately apportioned to you for specific, if unknown, reasons. You must do this well.
- You must testify that you are a Christian the way the original Christians did, through love and compassion. Some 2,000 years ago, in a world where a ruler could arbitrarily order the deaths of male children two years and younger before their disbelieving parent's eyes, in a world where men fought to the

death as amusement for the masses, they showed love and compassion toward each other. You must do the same.

- You will be required to do things, often minor, to testify to your faith. John 9:7 tells us of Jesus requiring a blind man to wash his eyes so he could see. Obviously, Jesus could grant sight regardless of any water. The entire point was that the person was required to do something to testify to their faith. The washing was purely symbolic, and our Lord was not only thinking of that man, but was most deliberately thinking of us in the twenty-first century. He was making a statement that those of us today must do things to testify to our faith. You may be asked by that distant voice in your conscience to do something to testify to your faith. You may feel the need to complement the janitor at work, allow a car to enter into your lane, or clean up after others. Regardless of how small, you will often be annoyed and inconvenienced by them. Regardless again, He wants you to do them as a testimony to Christianity as your way of life.

- You must ask for God's blessing, direction, approval, and guidance for your path. The lame man Jesus met by the pool was asked if he wanted to be well. The man had to ask; you must also ask.

- The freedom of will He bestowed on you can also be the freedom to reject His will. Prisons are full of those who cast aside God's will for them. Ephesians 5:15-17 says, "Be very careful, then, how you live – not as unwise but as wise, making the most of every opportunity, because the days are evil. Therefore, do not be foolish, but understand what the Lord's will is." This should be a daily thought.

- You will often be unsure of your path, but you can trust that God's plans for you are based on His absolute love for you. You must put in the one foundation puzzle piece of trust in Him, regardless of how weakly you add it. He will then add many, many more pieces to your puzzle for you when you do so.

- A key foundation puzzle piece that God inserts for you is that you have an advocate in the Holy Spirit. You may rarely think or call upon Him, but His presence will be a constant in your life regardless. John 14:16-17 tells us, "And I will ask the Father, and he will give you another advocate to help you and be with you forever – the Spirit of truth. The world cannot accept him because it neither sees nor knows him. But you know him, for he lives with you and will be in you." It is crucial that when Jesus speaks of the Holy Spirit, He refers to Him as the "Spirit of truth."

- The unexpected is the expected in the world of the Holy Spirit. Lives and history will be changed as a result of His actions. The great Christian apologist C.S. Lewis began as a confirmed atheist. Paul set out to Damascus to annihilate Christianity. The Christian writer Thomas Merton had someone come from India simply to tell him to read St. Augustine's *Confessions*. The twentieth-century theologian Dorothy Sayers committed adultery with a married man and had a child out of wedlock before coming to the Lord. Puzzle pieces may be inserted unknowingly by you or unexpectedly by God. Expect that.

- Your actions, words, and thoughts will occasionally come directly from God. He simply needs something done and you will serve as His tool for the moment. It may be intended for you, but just as likely for someone else. You will wonder where on earth you got an idea or what possessed you to do or say such a thing. It was not from earth.

- The Lord deliberately used the plural "plans" in Jeremiah 29:11. You will find yourself with many phases in your life, often based on earlier ones, yet independent in their own right. Like a prism, you will have many facets to your life – family, religious, work, social, etc., each reflecting the light of the others and forming the beacon that you are to follow. Your prism can cast a white light or a darkened shade. If darkness follows or comes from you, the puzzle pieces comprising your current life may have been put together wrong or are misunderstood. Often, we try to force pieces together as we want them to be, not as they should be. Disassembly of these can hurt our heart, but we must rearrange our lives at times. These are multiple puzzle pieces.

- God has made a lifetime of plans for us and many seem to require we feel certain emotions. Major events in our lives almost by definition hold an emotional component. He seems to require that we experience almost all human emotions possible during our lives. Why He wants that is beyond human understanding, but can be dealt with by having trust. Proverbs 3:5-6 informs us, "Trust in the Lord with all your heart and lean not on your own understanding; in all your ways submit to him, and he will make your paths straight."

- Your specific life will be immensely unfair. Those moments of unfairness will provide foundation puzzle pieces you may use to strengthen the outer border of your Life Puzzle. You can also choose to not add them. You will be stronger if you add them.

- There will be times satan will attempt to grasp you for their purposes. However, on those occasions, the emotions you feel at that time – pride, anger, envy, lust, or greed - can tell you the source. Being in tune with your emotions, especially around others, can provide vital puzzle pieces.

- You will be attacked by satan throughout your life. Further, satan will attack you daily, notably early in the day, and also around family, coworkers, and friends. Your emotions are often his most effective weapon. They will be the battleground. Your thoughts and the thoughts of those near you will be known to satan. Pitting people against each other by influencing thoughts and emotions are his tactics. Understanding this warfare is a puzzle piece.

- Your only ally and hope in this warfare are God and His mercy. Upon asking for it (and you must ask), you will receive it and in accordance with your needs. It will almost always seem inadequate, but will be sufficient. You grow spiritual muscles by exercising what you are given. 1 Corinthians 10:13 reassures us, "No temptation has overtaken you except what is common to mankind. And God is faithful; he will not let you be tempted beyond what you can bear. But when you are tempted, he will also provide a way out so that you can endure it." That way out may involve honesty, integrity, or having high moral standards.

- Additional foundation puzzle pieces are the core set of beliefs central to all Christians, including the Bible being God's sacred, infallible word, and acceptance of Jesus as the Son of God and your savior. There are also many additional and sometimes conflicting beliefs. Some denominations hold you must confess your sins to a priest to have them removed. Some baptize via immersion while others sprinkle. Some state alcohol is forbidden, likewise dancing. Still, others decry the use of modern medical services. God's path for you will be within the core beliefs. He may also guide you in regards to the other aspects and beliefs in Christendom.

- An additional foundation puzzle piece is the understanding that God has different timings than mortals. God's timing will typically be slower than what you will want. God's processes rarely seem to be straight lines in our myopic eyes. A long-involved series of steps often occurs before an outcome and its impact on all. God's timing will be perfect for what He wants; however, you may put things off too long and miss opportunities you were meant to take. God seems to like it when you are prepared and act instead of delay things to the point of loss.

- Another foundation puzzle piece is knowing that one of God's greatest miracles is that He loves you when you are your most unlovable. He may be embarrassed and ashamed by your actions and words. You don't just break His laws; you break His heart. Regardless, He loves and will forgive you if you ask.

- An odd foundation puzzle piece is the belief by almost all humans that they could move mountains if they only had someone move the foothills out of their way first. Regarding that near-universal belief, you should know that you will move a great many foothills in your life and the mountains will know of it. Normally, you will not know how mighty your work was until Jesus shows you in paradise. Raising a Christian child, not cheating on your taxes, serving decades in church volunteer roles, spending many hours caring for your cancer-stricken sister, and not lying to a police officer while they question you about your car accident, are all foothills. Jesus will see them as mountains and bless you for them.

These are some of the foundation puzzle pieces you can add as a second layer behind your Life Puzzle's outer border. Many more may be placed in your life as God sees the need for you to have them. The ones listed will be woven throughout this book and the remainder of your years. They will serve as touchstones for Christianity for the remainder of your life.

Christianity as a Way of Life

A large part in the center of our puzzle is a section showing that Christianity is not only a set of God-decreed truths, but that Christianity is a way of life predicated upon these truths. This way of life was promised to you in Jeremiah as a way of hope and a future, a way of prosperity, not of harm.

In embracing Christianity as a way of life, you will discover that it permeates into all facets of your life. There is a synergistic power that invades when one deliberately works at making Christianity a means and way of living. In people on this path, warmth, honesty, and integrity are radiated and enrich the lives of those surrounding them.

Each path will be different; each path will belong to God. In life we will find ourselves enticed by various interests, pleasures, and joys. We will find ourselves in despair, abandoned, and lost. We will find much, but throughout, we can find ourselves living Christianity as a way of life.

We may well have our eyes affixed toward God in heaven, but it is on earth we have been assigned His work. John 17:18 enriches us, "As you sent me into the world, I have sent them into the world."

On my personal trek, I found my way of life involved being drawn toward Christianity, family, public speaking, writing, and computers. I went through situations at work, in friendships, and with my family that carved deep grooves with a dull blade on my soul. I met Murphy's Law, "Anything that can go wrong will," and determined that Murphy was a raving optimist. I've been dumbfounded by my blessings from the Holy Spirit and found myself in abject despair. Yet, throughout my life, there was that cornerstone of Christ in my life. I relied on God and knew that

His path for my life is based on His overwhelming love for me regardless of how poorly I managed my life and situations.

You will be guided in building your Life Puzzle through understanding the abilities and interests you have, the people who influence you, circumstances you find yourself in, and the experiences you will undergo. You will be body-slammed by life and be triumphant in work, social life, family, and school. Completely unexpected things will happen as the Holy Spirit works through you.

As you put together puzzle pieces, you will glimpse the path built specifically for you by Him. You can make your first few steps on this path of Christianity as a way of life. Fathers are proud when their children make their first steps, including Our Father.

You can make more steps as you deliberately live Christ's teachings, knowing that this requires the enabling presence of the Holy Spirit. As your actions, thoughts, and behaviors begin to align with what God intended for you more closely, a peace bordering on serenity will be bestowed. You will find rest for your weary and burdened soul. Your yoke will become easy, and your life burdens lighter.

When people encounter a person living Christianity as a way of life, they almost never realize them for what they are. They commonly see that person as having a warm personality, a confidence about them, a positive attitude, possessing a low-key self-assurance, having poise, is trustworthy, exudes honesty and integrity, and they have an aura that attracts others. People are attracted to them, but typically do not understand why.

As you take your first steps in living Christianity as a way of life, you will also encounter opposition to you and your path for no other reason than many in the world oppose Christianity. The world and satan will assault you. At times you will be scorned, laughed at, rejected, and even hated. But you will find consolation in John 15:18 where Jesus tells us, "If the world hates you, keep in mind that it hated me first."

Puzzle Pieces

Consider the following:
- Which of the listed foundation puzzle pieces are most apparent in your life? What do they mean to you?

- What are some additional foundation puzzle pieces that have entered your life?
- What foundation puzzle pieces will be added to your life in the next year?
- What does Christianity as a way of life mean to you?
- What steps will you perform this week to testify to Christianity being your way of life?

4. Critical Junctions (The Workings of the Holy Spirit Writ Large)

Critical junctions are the special and significant work of the Holy Spirit in your life.

From the beginning of my Christian trek, it was instilled in me that God acted in our lives. God the Father, God the Son, and God the Holy Spirit were combined in the great mystery of the Holy Trinity as the one and only true God. Things occurred in our lives, and I was told this was the handiwork of the Holy Spirit, both one of three and the one and only.

If you maintain that God the Father, instead of God the Holy Spirit, sets these things in motion, all is well. He is God with the three and the one in perfect balance. His will is seen through the events, thoughts, and actions that occur in our brief lives. God can and does act decisively in our lives, and, given my background, I will speak of the Holy Spirit in regards to critical junctions.

Critical Junctions

Critical Junctions are those events that change the trajectory of your life. Caused or allowed to happen by the Holy Spirit, your life will change. Selected people will be interjected into your life, writings, or other media will impact you, thoughts will occur, and circumstances will change. Your life's trajectory will be altered by these twists and coincidences. They may change it profoundly or simply introduce a minor correction, but change it they will. Critical junctions can occur from people, writings, dreams, words of wisdom, assignments at work, and the happenstances of daily life. They can be a death in the family, a new job in a strange city, or the chance meeting of your future spouse. They can be a delay in leaving home that prevents you from being in a car accident. They can be a minor skill learned at work that catapults your career. They are many, and they are God's deflections and reflections. Our future is shaped by these events that occur or are bypassed in our lives. God seems to use these to direct and instruct us. Sometimes they are brutally inflicted upon us, but often we are allowed to accept or reject them. They can be seen as miracles or the exact opposite. More often, they are considered blips on our radar to which we react. Frequently we do not recognize them for what they are when they occur or maybe never recognize them.

They may show themselves through unexpected turns of events or sets of coincidences. They may be what we saw coming down the pipe, but we were hoping the pipe would spring a leak before reaching us. They may be certain situations we had prayed for or were dreading. They may also occur when you find yourself saying or doing things and wondering where on earth they came from. They may not be coming from earth. The good, the bad, the ugly, and the beautiful in life can all be found in critical junctions.

An opportunity may ring once, or adversity may seem permanently pressing on your front doorbell. As Lawrence J. Peters put it, "Fortune knocks but once. Misfortune has much more patience." Both will be deliberately placed in your life.

As noted earlier, you will receive an advocate, the Holy Spirit. You may rarely think or call upon Him, but He will be with you, and He will place critical junctions in your life.

History teaches that the unexpected is the expected in the world of the Holy Spirit. Lives may well be altered in unforeseen ways. My favorite example is the great Christian apologist C.S. Lewis who began his spiritual trek as a dedicated atheist determined to disprove Christianity. He died one of the most influential Christian writers of the last century.

Other critical junctions are seen in the Bible. The newborn Moses was placed in a basket and was saved by a princess. Joseph had a dream to take Mary and flee that very night to Egypt. A small shepherd, with no military training, walked with a sling to fight a huge warrior. Paul had his conversion on his way to Damascus to annihilate the expanding Christian movement. Critical junctions occurred, and human history was sent permanently down a different path.

We can, usually in retrospect, see these critical junctions in our lives and the lives of others. We can identify those twists and coincidences that changed, or could have changed, the course of our lives. To take these paths often requires a leap of faith. Robert Venditto is quoted as saying, "Throughout history, the most common debilitating human ailment has been cold feet." Through prayer, the counsel of others, and knowing what gifts, traits, abilities, and weaknesses we have, we make our best decision, act, and then leave the results in God's hands. The Bible is full of stories of actions born of faith, and history is comprised of those who made the best decisions they could with what they knew and felt.

One such critical junction occurred in my family before I was born. My father tore a knee ligament while in the army. As that it was very much a marching army at the time, he was given a medical discharge. His small unit of communications specialists was among the first to be sent to the Korean War, where every single member was soon killed. A critical junction occurred, and he was spared.

Prior to that, my father had been offered a minor league baseball contract, which he turned down. He confided in me that he always regretted his decision. A critical junction occurred, and a decision, rightly or wrongly, was made.

A series of critical junctions occurred in my life soon after college. After receiving my degree, I was at a party with friends, and I found myself blurting out that I would be moving to Texas to pursue my career to both my and everyone else's amazement. Doing my research, I decided that it could be a good move for my career, although I was unprepared for the roller coaster that would follow. In brief, after moving to Dallas, I was unable to gain employment in my field, but entered a different field where I met friends who helped launch me on my Christian trek. On a visit back to a friend in Missouri, I was smitten by a woman I met and moved to their town. From there, I found a job in Kansas City and met friends of my friends in Dallas and built a life there with them, progressed on my Christian path, but left the woman I came to Missouri for.

I often wondered if the Holy Spirit had me blurt out those words at the party to start my path toward Him.

Similarly, my career in training and writing came from the necessity to teach fellow employees how to use those newfangled microcomputers I was placing on their desks. I had no background in training or writing, but almost two decades as a programmer assisting newbies on PCs led to a long career in training and documentation.

Another junction occurred when a chance encounter with an AC repairman led to a friendship. Further, taking a class from a dynamic instructor I was ambivalent about, led to my developing an award-winning training style.

Will these always be positive experiences? A job I was certain I wanted and lobbied hard for became one of the worst experiences of my life. I was blinded by the money I could make and blinder still to the actual work I would be doing. I apparently needed to be blind-sided to learn a specific lesson.

Critical junctions can often be seen in coincidences in timing. Time is so valuable that God Himself seems to divvy it out in exact portions to mesh with another person's time and attention. The exact timing that allowed me to meet my future wife clearly served in that regard. Timing is that stuff of consequence.

Still, at other times, critical junctions are a profound and undeniable miracle. A minister of mine, in his first pastoral position, became familiar with a woman who had inoperable cancer. As her family was preparing for her to enter hospice care, God worked a miracle by totally removing the cancer from her body. The doctors were astonished as the tumor disappeared.

At these select junctions, we may find that our plans are forced to change, often unexpectedly. Sometimes we can attribute them to changes in technology, other times to a changing culture, and at still others to a marketing whim by a company. Regardless, these changes occur, and we can feel blindsided by the event and the speed with which we are forced to react.

Examples could include:
- Technology advancements forcing us to change our job skills
- An illness that brings together or disperses the family
- The unexpected divorce of parents or from your spouse
- A chance encounter with someone who later becomes your spouse

- An unplanned pregnancy
- A minor background in an area that leads to a new career in a new field

God intensely loves us and will, if we let Him, work in our lives and send us people, circumstances, thoughts, words, and decisions at critical junctions. Often, we will not recognize them at the time, but occur they will.

We can be caught flat-footed or be well primed for possibilities that may occur. At work, we can be equipped for changes looming on the horizon, or we can be completely blindsided. It has been said that chance favors the prepared. I would say that when it rains manna, be the one who purchased a large bowl a month earlier.

Opportunities will be presented in your life. Opportunities are never wasted. The other guy takes the opportunities you don't.

Sometimes a critical junction may occur with absolutely no warning. A woman I knew told me of a white-water rafting accident where one of her party flipped out of their rubber raft. She held on to her friend in a death grip while the others said to let go, and she would go under the raft and could get to the shore. No one thought of the current dragging her under. Instead, my friend pulled her up with a strength she did not have into the raft. Her arm all but came out of its socket, but she very well may have saved her companion's life. There was only time to react - and pray.

A vice president of a company I once worked for told the tale of a critical junction when his life was in dire jeopardy. He and two others were in a jeep driving down a jungle path during the Viet Nam war. They were beset by sniper fire and veered off the path into the jungle. Deciding their best hope was to drive back the way they came, the three picked the jeep up and turned it around. Jumping in, they drove back onto the path and made a wild dash back to their base.

Recounting their story, their comrades were astounded that the three could pick up the jeep, let alone rotate it to point it back to the path. So, the three attempted the task again and could not even begin to lift it. It simply weighed too much. The Holy Spirit had intervened and given them the strength needed for a brief critical junction.

Of all aspects of our lives, critical junctions may be the hardest to pinpoint and probably have the greatest degree of rejection. Our self-will can scuttle the best-laid plans that the Lord has for us. We are often given a choice, if not time, in these situations, and often our emotional reaction is the deciding factor. Your initial emotional response is usually a good determinant of how you should act, but a prayer, internal debate, and advice from a trusted friend can be vital, if time allows. But often, there is only time for a quick prayer.

What is often not recognized is that satan relishes these as prime opportunities and will attack us at these critical junctions. In these, we are often caught off guard and vulnerable to thoughts of anger, envy, and greed. We can find ourselves thinking that things should have gone better for us, that the situation is unfair, or that we deserved something and had better get it. Know that satan could not care less about the situation. He is simply seeking an opportunity to attack our emotions and agitate our relations with others.

What is worse, these attacks can be subtle and seemingly innocuous. In C.S. Lewis' *The Screwtape Letters*, he wrote of a man who reached a minor critical junction. He found himself reading spiritual material that was starting to have an impact on him when satan interjected the thought that he needed to have something to eat first and could get back to the material later. That later never came, and the decision to set aside the spiritual material was decisive. The episode was closed, and he lost what he was called upon to learn.

It must be noted that a critical junction can also be something that doesn't occur. Swerving to miss another car due to our texting can serve as a critical junction if we learn to not text and drive. A good scare is always better than good advice.

A few years ago, a fellow member told a church group I belonged to of a critical junction where something should have occurred, but didn't. A fireman he knew owned a house that had one room heated by a coal-burning stove. Above it hung a picture of Jesus. He sold the house, and in taking down the picture, he found a large scorch mark. The vent inside the wall had ruptured and burned through the wall. The back of the picture was likewise scorched. Being a fireman, he knew there was no possible way that flames hadn't consumed the house. Likewise, the front of the picture should have been as scorched as the back had been. The Lord had worked a small miracle at a critical junction and spared his home and family.

Minor Critical Junctions

Critical junctions may be minor, but memorable. We may blurt out something and have no idea why we said it or a minor incident might cause a slight trajectory change in our lives.

Some years ago, I pulled out into traffic in front of a pickup pulling a large trailer that couldn't stop in time and was hit. There was no damage to his truck and minor damage to my car. He was upset, but out of the blue, he asked me if I was a Christian. I told him I was a very strong Christian. He replied that we should then forget the whole thing. I thanked him in the name of the Lord.

About two years later, a driver, who was not watching me come to a halt at a light, rear-ended me, causing no damage to our cars. They seemed frightened and deeply worried. The earlier episode flashed through my mind, and I asked them if they were a Christian. They said they were, so I said we can forget the entire thing. He was clearly relieved, and we went our different ways. The Holy Spirit provided minor critical junctions in both occasions, and both reaffirmed Christianity as a way of life.

Critical junctions may test our morals and convictions and can occur in an eye blink. That Christmas gift someone left in a shopping cart in the parking lot is there for the taking, a chance to lie and get out of a work meeting is tempting, and the option to skip out of the kid's birthday party are all available, and all must be decided upon in a heartbeat. Those heartbeats must belong to God.

I suspect that we occasionally blurt out things for no reason other than what seems to be for the Holy Spirit's amusement. My father, as a Boy Scout leader, was told that Boy Scouts shake with their left hand because, in days of old, warriors had to drop their shields to do so. Therefore, only the bravest of the brave shook with their left hands. My father instantaneously replied, "That or the dumbest of the dumb." Perhaps it was my father's quick wit, or perhaps it was for the Holy Spirit's mirth. Regardless, it became part of family lore.

We learn His will for us not only from what we were given in mental, spiritual, and physical gifts and defects, but the types of critical junctions placed in our lives. We can see serendipitous and direct interjections of the Holy Spirit through interactions, writings, dreams, advice, and

61

happenstances. These junctions can be as simple as learning a quote we later use for guidance. "You can tell more about a person by what he says about others than you can by what others say about him," by Audrey Hepburn has served me well in that regard. They may be as complex as starting your own business. They can be tragic with an unexpected family death, or they can be euphoric with the announcement of a pregnancy. They can be anything, but they are meant to steer your life's path and to instruct you in His ways.

Puzzle Pieces

Consider the following:

- Name three events that changed the trajectory of your youth. They could be a school subject, making a best friend, your family moving, or the divorce of your parents.
- Name three events that changed the course of your adulthood. Possibilities include a new job, a marriage, the birth of your first child, a forced move to another city, buying a house, or health issues.
- How do you think God was trying to direct you with your critical junctions? How did they impact the trajectory of your life? How would your life be different today if they had not occurred?
- Can you see possible future critical junctions coming regarding work, family, finances, or health issues? How are you prepared for them?
- What are some minor critical junctions that seem to have nudged the direction of your life? An interest in a hobby or activity? Making a friendship? A car accident? A job transfer?

5. Your Fellow Man

Humans are not a particularly loving species, but we seem meant to be close to our fellow man in actions and emotions. I will freely admit that I would rather pass a kidney stone than an hour with some people. Still others, I could easily spend a full day with and wish it had been longer.

The Bible tells us that whenever two or more are gathered in His name, He is there. Why does the Bible dictate two or more? There must be a need to be with our fellow man. There must be a need to be with our fellow believers.

Proverbs 27:17 tells us, "As iron sharpens iron, so one person sharpens another." And we are very much sharpened, amused, dismayed, encouraged, and disheartened by Adam's progeny. From family, to close friendships, to acquaintances, to strangers, God seems to have decreed that we need to walk alongside our fellow man.

I once heard that if you learn one good thing from every book you read, class you take, or person you spend much time with, you are way ahead of the game. I'm not certain what game they were referring to, but it seems quite true that we can learn about our predestined path, whether directly or through osmosis, by merely spending time with our fellow human beings.

Nowhere can we be influenced more serendipitously than in our dealings with others. As we spend our decades rubbing elbows and egos with our fellow man, we develop the calluses we call life experiences. Life experiences dictate we need to test the waters when interacting with others. Over time we learn trust and confidence in dealing with our fellow, struggling human beings. At times we are disappointed, yet at others, we receive a windfall of good experiences. Regardless, the Lord occasionally places specific others in our lives for distinct purposes that we may not recognize until much later.

We soon realize we can't predict a person's impact on our lives by their profession or family. A minister's son I met was a terror. A minister I knew was an alcoholic. A recovered alcoholic was among the kindest people I ever met, and a teacher I was ambivalent toward served as a pattern for the type of teacher I would become. Predictions go out the window quickly.

A question that we must ask ourselves is if we were given good role models for our interactions with others. Were we taught well about marriage, parenting, and making friendships? If not, then we may find ourselves in the unenviable position of having to discover how to interact with others. We may find ourselves guessing at what normal is and attempting to mimic the behavior of others who have spouses, families, and friends. We may find ourselves gravitating toward others who are or are not good role models for us. We may find ourselves manipulated by those who sense our social ineptness. We may be guided by those who are living Christianity as their way of life. At the very least, we should have enough God-given common sense to not learn role model behaviors from TV sitcoms.

It seems a truism that at some time in our lives, we will know a person whom we will wonder if they are an angel in human disguise. And we will also know a person whom we would move mountains for merely for the opportunity to sit on their snout and fart. Yet we are commanded to love both.

C.S. Lewis gave us the guidance we need, "Do not waste time bothering whether you 'love' your neighbor; act as if you did. As soon as we do this, we find one of the great secrets. When you are behaving as if you loved someone, you will presently come to love them."

Differences

Obviously, the Lord made us in many racial and ethnic groups. In the American melting pot, we actively work, serve, and live alongside others of many races, religions, sexual orientations, and ethnicities. Although white, I am in the minority in my office and genuinely enjoy my time with my coworkers. In the Bible, Jesus showed us through His examples that we should interact with others different than ourselves. He initiated the conversation with the Samaritan woman at the well, regardless that Jews and Samaritan's did not associate with each other. Jesus healed the Roman centurion's servant and the Canaanite woman's daughter. Some Biblical scholars feel the feeding of the four thousand included Gentiles.

Today, much of the racism that has divided our country seems to be diminishing, but at a much slower pace than I would have anticipated. I was born the year after the Supreme Court struck down segregation and lived to see the first African-American president and interracial dating and marriage become acceptable to the large majority of Americans. The more racist elements of society seem to be dwindling, but notably hardened cases remain. I remember the most racist person I ever met. He swore that you shouldn't sell alcohol to Indians or pickups to African-Americans. He claimed that the former simply couldn't handle alcohol, and the latter would automatically think of all things they could steal once they had a pickup. He was regarded as something of a stupid joke by all races around him.

In every human who has ever existed, from Adam through a new human being conceived at this very moment, we can see distinct differences. Height, weight, intelligence, race, ethnicity, constitution, skills, aptitude, attitude, emotions, and the differences engraved on us from the second by second experiences of our lives. Add to that human culture, social mores, family influence, and the gamut of personal beliefs, and it is absolutely guaranteed that no two humans have ever been the same, nor will ever be the same. Some things are as obvious as can be.

And we couldn't be more wrong.

We are looking through the blindness inherent in all things human. Worse, satan himself is working to slit our eyes open with a rusty blade – and often succeeds. There is one thing that is rarely thought of because of its obviousness.

We have a common denominator. At the most bedrock level, we are souls. That is what God sees. A quote frequently attributed to C.S. Lewis put it best, "You do not have a soul. You are a soul. You have a body."

Nothing we will ever do will make our soul grow larger. At no time can we expand upon what we were given at conception. It is impossible to diminish it, share it with another, or borrow part of your neighbor's. Yes, our lifetime of deeds and words will be associated with it (deeds and words Jesus personally redeemed us of), but the soul itself is the soul itself.

65

Did God grant those of a particular race or ethnic background a different sized soul and, therefore, some are superior in God's eyes? For a brief moment, let's consider this absurdity to be true.

If He did, who would he have given an extended, extra-large version soul to? To answer that, we need to ask who He directly and deliberately came to for many millennia. Who did He call his chosen people? Who did He have his only begotten Son walk in the flesh among so that they would hear His words, receive His miracles, and touch His garment?

It was the Jewish race and some Gentiles of the middle east. The middle east is where the Old Testament took place. The middle east was also the location of the New Testament, save for a few mentions of Rome and Greece. Those residing at that time in China, India, Iceland, Mexico, Brazil, England, Ireland, Australia, Germany, North America, South Africa, and the rest did not make the cut. Further, the Romans served primarily to crucify God's beloved Son.

Those who lived in the middle east, with notably dark skin (an inconvenient truth to some), were the ones Jesus appeared to, performed miracles for, selected as apostles, and whom He built His church upon. They alone heard His words, and they alone were personally blessed by Him.

It is clear. It is obvious. Wouldn't the souls of those with middle eastern genetics and dark skin be more robust, beautiful, and glorious? The Romans were the only western Europeans in the New Testament, and they served to mock, scorn, and torture our Lord. Wouldn't God inflict a wretched sliver of a soul on those of European descent and pale skin for the suffering and murder of his Son?

Nowhere in the Bible is there even a remote indication that people are given different souls based on race, ethnicity, or any other imaginary difference.

Instead, what the sacred word of God says, and it is the last command given by Christ Himself before His Ascension, is that we are to make disciples of all nations. We are to teach them of God and His Son. We are to baptize all nations without exception in His name.

We must see others as God sees us - as souls. We must treat each other as the same. We are the same. We are souls, not the dust that our containers will return to in a trifling few decades.

The Great Commission, the last words from Jesus to the human race, can be seen as the tangent point between God and those of us living today as Christians. He could have told the disciples those words early in His ministry. Instead, because of their immense importance, He chose to end His earthly ministry with that last command to us as He pushed our boat out to sea. A boat deliberately filled with Jews, Arabs, Africans, Hispanics, Caucasians, Chinese, Indians, and all the other souls God created.

So then, does that Asian woman at work own a soul that would balance on the scale precisely to yours in God's eyes? Does the black man with cancer own what God values the most to the exact amount as yours? Does the white person sitting in a prison cell possess a soul bestowed to them of the same make and model as yours? When we denigrate another, we show contempt and scorn to God Himself for the only thing He wants from us - our souls. It only serves to delight satan, for it is also the only thing he wants from us.

Interacting with Others

You may decide not to interact, let alone establish friendships, with others outside of your political persuasion, mindset, culture, race, religion, or nationality. Certainly, you are not harming these others by being sequestered with your own.

But did Jesus segregate Himself with his Jewish clan? Did Jesus go to and speak to the Samaritan woman, despite the hard fact that Jews and Samaritans never interacted? Did Jesus deliberately use a Samaritan, who were considered unclean and fiercely hated by Jews, as the hero in His story of the Good Samaritan (with a priest and Levite leaving a gravely injured man to die)?

Did Jesus initiate contacts with sinners and tax collectors? Did He heal the Roman centurion's servant, full knowing that Roman soldiers, possible reporting to that man, would spit on Him, scorn Him, and drive nails into His hands and feet?

In insulating ourselves from those who are different, are we following His example?

If we separate our lives from others, can we serve as examples to them of Christianity as our way of life? By isolating ourselves from others, will they be able to see the power and influence of Christ in our lives? Does banishing those considered undesirable by us leave us as Christians in a closet where no one can see His impact on us in the dark?

Homeless men, women with mental illness, children who smell because of no shower in their homes, elderly who lost all to scammers, alcoholics, meth addicts, immigrants to the land of immigrants, and so many more have lives we want nothing to do with. Yet, these were the ones Jesus deliberately went to. They are the ones we can at least speak civilly to, donate to charities for, buy a present for on a Christmas angel tree, and serve a meal to at a shelter this weekend.

Those of a different political persuasion, nationality, culture, or race may be even more hated than those just listed, but did Jesus hate those in His day that were different in these ways? Even when He knew those were the ones who would torment and slaughter Him in the evilest way they knew how?

The point is that He commanded us with His words and actions to not confine ourselves to those like us, who agree with our politics, or think as we do. He went to those who would torture and kill Him. And He did it out of love. We must also interact with others who are different. It is our duty, and it is a duty directly to Him.

Our Initial Family

Our first interactions with others come within our family with all its inherent dynamics. It is called the nuclear family owing to its explosive potential. We find ourselves helpless and frail, nurtured by our parents, and entirely dependent on them. As we grow, we begin to interact differently with them and make our demands known to whoever is in earshot of our two-year-old screaming voices. We then learn what we are told is for our own good – an increasing dose of discipline with an attendant larger dose of love. Amazingly we survive.

Our family will guide our path, and we will probably not question it – initially. As we grow, we need to learn of God and His overwhelming love for us. From there, we discover church, religion, and faith. We are laying the foundation for finding the path God has set forth for us and Christianity as our way of life.

What we learn and integrate into our character from parents, siblings, and extended family members may be the most critical determinant in defining the specific path we will follow. Our family's way of life, and how we were raised is often more important than what life hurls at us. Using that backdrop, we attempt to decide our future, education, work, spouse, adult family, and how we are to live out our days. Regardless of what we choose in those areas, we are influenced profoundly by how we were raised, and our actions will display that influence.

Stability is a vital factor. Was there a nurturing, stable family life or instability and turmoil? Did you frequently move between cities and schools? Did your parent's work careers affect you? Did a parent's divorce scar you? Did you feel you could count on a parent or relative to support and protect you from the world? The answers are part of what defines you.

Often it isn't until we are adults that we realize that we were our parent's favorite child, just another one of the kids, or the "lost child" who simply did not fit into the family well. Stability issues and your position as a child will impact your attitude toward life and how you interpret the many guideposts God places in your life.

Typically, families have unwritten rules you are to abide by. Families I have known have had rules including that they worry, but don't talk about money, affection is not to be given except to very small children, they keep quiet about troubles regardless of how obvious they are, and that whatever upsets mother will change from moment to moment and is totally forbidden to do.

These rules will impact your outlook on life and toward others. You may integrate them into your spirit or rebel against them. Regardless, they will affect you.

Your Adult Family

Marriage and founding a family are normal life course events. Our spouse, children, in-laws, and, possibly, our ex's all play significant roles in each day's activities, decisions, emotions, and thoughts.

Some claim that the American family has deteriorated in the past few generations. Perhaps, but what divorce does to families today, death did for centuries. Average life spans up until the 1800s hovered in the thirties.

Dan Boozan

Adults often lost their spouse to disease or death in childbirth. The extended family's social network was called upon to make up for this loss, or a marriage of convenience was arranged.

We may not have the time we would like for our children today, but children of yesteryear often were one of many and received little individual attention. The man who came to America and founded my family some one-hundred and fifty years ago also founded ten children by his first wife, who presumably died of exhaustion, and seven by his second wife. The idea of spending quality time with each of seventeen children was a nonstarter. Children of yesteryear made do with little "quality time" with their parents. Today, much of our quality time is spent in the car as we shuffle our children between activities.

Regardless, our family can survive and thrive.

Marriage

One of my favorite quotes is, "A man is incomplete until he is married. Then he's finished." This quote comes to us courtesy of one of the great supporters of marriage in our era, Zsa Zsa Gabor.

As ancient as Adam is the concept of marriage and pairing together. Genesis 2:18 tells us, "The Lord God said, 'It is not good for the man to be alone. I will make a helper suitable for him.'" Then He brought Eve forth from him, and the first rocky relationship began.

Like that first couple, your life plans are inexorably intertwined. Your spouse may well be the single most crucial factor in your emotional and physical health. They will have a profound influence on your path. Long after your children leave the nest, they will remain.

It has been said that marriage is a seventy/thirty percent proposition with each side giving the seventy percent. I will not argue the math but will argue that leaving the relationship leaves one proportionally less than what God decreed one should be.

Further, it has been said that marriage is a triumph over differing personalities, a triumph over lifestyles, and a triumph over common sense. But regardless, a marriage is a triumph. No wonder people applaud when a couple announces their thirtieth or greater anniversary.

I was once told that a key factor in marital success is having a joint interest with your spouse outside of your children. To those considering this brave new world, they would do well to consider what they will share in addition to family matters. Do they enjoy church activities, sports, renovating houses, travel, gardening, cooking, reading, hiking, or the thousands of other activities open to them? Having both partners check mark two or more of such could be significant as they serve as foundation blocks for not only marriage, but for the deep friendship that must be established between the two.

Along our life path in the marriage process, we find that keeping the lines of communication open is paramount. Time in quantity is required, with lengthy discussions imperative. With our spouse, we share hopes, dreams, triumphs, and our deepest and most personal thoughts. We also share gossip, annoyances, trivia, and confusion. We come together and have in-laws we miscommunicate with together, have children we misunderstand together, and have friends we misread together that makes our togetherness a joy. It is the "you never," "I always," and "who brought the subject up first," which bring us marital bliss. All are needed, all are required, and all are part of marriage.

Having experienced the husband component of marriage, having friends who are husbands, and having read on the role and importance of being a husband I have noted fundamental changes that occur in both partners in this institution.

Upon saying "I do," the DNA of the now husband and wife are permanently biochemically altered.

A wife's DNA at that point will generate a cross-referenced, comprehensive database as a permanently anchored pop up on her visual screen of life. It contains all mistakes made by their husband going back to before he was born. The screen continuously updates so as to generate the nastiest reminders of his past failures, quirks, idiosyncrasies, and shortcomings, regardless that there is no correlation to any words or activity by him at that moment. It is the quantum computer system that male computer scientists are attempting to create, but with no hope of duplicating that which women are conferred with upon walking down the aisle.

Correcting their spouse on any and all actions and words seems to release dopamine into their system resulting in feelings of well-being, pleasure, and a mild euphoria. Overdosing on this pleasure inducing action is common and to be expected.

The husband's DNA, upon kissing his bride, (the DNA transformation for both apparently occurs at this point) descends into an aquatic level whereby they, like goldfish, have a three second memory of things their wives have done wrong in their relationship. That may be the key as to why wives insist upon keeping husbands around.

In summary, to my friends serving in the minor role of husbands, wives are more sarcastic, bad-tempered, nasty, and cantankerous than we can ever be. And they live longer.

Regardless of any altered DNA sequences, marriage is one of the most important steps we take on God's path for us.

Children

If children come along, then the Lord's path may turn from a leisurely stroll into running the hurdles. Maintaining your composure becomes a whimsical afterthought as your little angel makes mud pies out of the kitty litter. You will find yourself the family garbage disposal as you eat the blackened bananas and expired food the kids didn't want. Regardless, you are learning survival skills as a parent and a little more of God's path for you.

As they grow, you will become the single most important person in their lives, and you will ponder on God's plan for your children and the hope and a future that He also promised them. You set their initial paths, their priorities, their emotional foundation, and their security.

Proverbs 22:6 is invaluable, "Start children off on the way they should go, and even when they are old, they will not turn from it." Your influence on their personality, morals, and ways of thinking will always be a part of what constitutes them throughout their lives. There are no guarantees; however, this Biblical admonition tells us how important we are to our children's development and direction throughout their lives.

Now, if we just had some control over that freedom of choice that they (like us at their age) seem irritatingly bent to use.

Teachers and School

At the advanced age of five, we are sent to school where most of us serve sixteen to twenty years or more of hard, unpaid labor. Your first lesson is that the other kids get allowances, but you don't. A lasting lesson is that life is innately unfair. Your last lesson is that there are probably no jobs, that you will want, awaiting you at graduation.

You may have had the good fortune to experience excellent teachers who encouraged and set time aside for you. You may never have had such a teacher. They may have been tough and demanding of your efforts or couldn't have cared less about your work.

My better teachers showed their concern for me in their insistence that I learn their topics and learn them well. Pop quizzes would consist of the question, "Prove to me you read the topic for today" or "Compare and contrast the two topics you should have learned last week." My best teachers forced me to think beyond what our textbooks contained. From a select few, I learned to question things, but to raise my hand first.

Regardless of your experiences, God may well have required you to take specific instructors to learn lessons in responsibility, dedication, time-management, and to press your mental limits. Often, we find these were the primary reasons we were meant to take such instructors, not the topics taught.

Having been a trainer for years, I know it is a truism that an instructor can learn much from their students. I have been on both sides of that exchange and been grateful for these. One memorable experience came while at college, in my Intro to Psychology class. My professor was dismissing Freud, saying that not much of his work was used in today's psychology. Without thinking, I blurted out, "His terminology is." He gave me a look like I was an unordered side dish. Awaiting a verbal body slam, I was amazed that he acknowledged to the room I was very much correct. I'm not sure he ever forgave me for that.

Ministers and their Spouses

Ministers and minister's spouses are two of the most vital, vulnerable, rewarding, influential, and attack inviting positions ever created. Both very much involve a calling, and both are very much expressions of God's love to mankind, even though the burden on these couples is immense, and often rewards (on earth) are meager.

We find God not only using them to instruct us through weekly sermons, but also in the activities inside our church family. Often, we are

73

active in our youth at our church, but are oblivious to the hours the adults, especially the pastor and their spouse, put in on our behalf. As we mature in our church, God normally calls on us, as part of our path, to take on responsibilities in education, overseeing children, providing music, assisting with Bible studies, preparing coffee, working on Christmas and Easter celebrations, and other needs. He provides us with an opportunity to grow in our faith through such activities. The decision is left with us. We can grow, stagnate, or even revert to a weaker faith. Our pastor and their spouse can assist in accelerating this growth, but we must do the growing.

A minister or their spouse may become a primary influence in your life if you allow them to. Their guidance can be a literal Godsend, but bear in mind the time and effort required of them. Pastors and their families have a direct calling from God, and that calling includes being pulled in fifty directions at once. Sometimes it is recognized with the minister, but rarely with their spouse, who can be pulled in a hundred directions. Work to get to know your minister and their family and serve your church's needs. Spiritual muscles are built here, and your life path will certainly go through here.

Understand that ministers and their spouses directly serve the Lord, and only another minister or minister's spouse can ever truly understand what it is like to be in these positions.

Hebrews 13:17 grants us guidance, "Have confidence in your leaders and submit to their authority because they keep watch over you as those who must give an account. Do this so that their work will be a joy, not a burden, for that would be of no benefit to you."

Mentors

The Lord may have decided that you will need a mentor in life. Part teacher, part friend, part devil's advocate they may help you traverse the inevitable bumps and bruises of life. Ideally, we will have many such advisors during our days. Proverbs 11:14 tells us, "For lack of guidance a nation falls, but victory is won through many advisors."

Some will have this expression of grace placed in our lives, and some will not. Those of us who do may not recognize such a blessing until it is gone. Rarely is a mentor a close family member, although an aunt or uncle who is concerned about you may well qualify. Work can provide a mentor in the guise of an older, more knowledgeable worker who takes an interest in us. Teachers can likewise fill this role.

Proverbs 20:18 guides us, "Plans are established by seeking advice; so if you wage war, obtain guidance." Life often seems like a war zone where we have found ourselves in enemy-occupied territory needing advice and more. Indeed, satan is the enemy on earth, and he does control much of the terrain.

Our path with a mentor may be tentative and occasional or headstrong and robust. Frequently it vacillates as your yoke is called upon to bear greater loads under their guidance. As your burden is increased, your mentor may lean away from you to teach you responsibility, or they may step in and give you explicit direction.

Your path may never see such a mentor, but you may be called upon, untrained, to serve in that role. It may press the limits of your patience, acceptance, and abilities, often for meager gratitude. Regardless, He may call upon you to serve in this manner. James Keller gives us perspective, "A candle loses nothing by lighting another candle."

Friends

You may have few friends, or you might make friends with anyone who can't defend themselves. You might be the one that others know to go to when trouble occurs, or your attitude might be, "A friend in need is a bum." Regardless, God wants us to have friends to share our lives with.

Friendship is described in Romans 12:10 (KJV), "Be kindly affectioned one to another with brotherly love; in honor preferring one another." Examples we are given include Job's friends, David and Jonathan, and Ruth and Naomi.

It is a fact of life that women do it better. They seem to make, grow, and retain friendships much better than us guys. Possibly this is due to the centuries where men were expected to be independent and were in competition with each other for jobs and means to support their families. Women, as a rule, stayed at home, nurtured the children, and met and became friends with neighboring women.

Today, friendships are often carryovers from our school days and kept on life support via Facebook, WhatsApp, WeChat, Instagram, Twitter, emails, etc. Life often seems too busy for face-to-face time, and we are poorer for it.

God places friends and potential friends in our lives at work, church, school, and social events to fill a distinct requirement. Comradery seems to be a necessity in life, one that fulfills a God-given innate need. God's plan for your life will be hollow without others to share trust, triumphs, and trials with.

Who wants to celebrate buying a new house in an empty new house?

We were meant to spend time studying together, helping move friends to their new home, bringing a birthday cake to a coworker, and helping others find their lost dog. It is hardly surprising that loneliness and a lack of social support have been linked to an increased risk of heart disease and cancer. (Friendship, n.d.) Some researchers even refer to friendship networks as a "behavioral vaccine" that boosts both physical and mental health. (Sias & Bartoo, 2007)

A friend can help you learn life skills, assist you in defining your priorities, give you a Christmas gift after you lost your job, and introduce you to your future spouse. They help you through illnesses, lessen depression, steer your life, and give you a blunt reality check - but with love. Their job description is complex, and different friends do it differently.

Forbearance on the order of Job may needed with some friends, while others are a delight to be near. One telling aspect of our personalities is the type of friends we seem to attract. I have a niece who is a true mosquito magnet and I seem to serve the same for neurotic talkers. I am the quiet type, yet for decades I have brought into my life those whose talk is better described as continuous eruptions. Long ago, in one memorable ten-hour session, I counted the seconds between discharges. A five second average was calculated with one extraordinary silence of fifteen seconds realized during that marathon. What others said to them was dismissed as irrelevant and the disjointed onslaught continued. I truly liked my friend, but I wondered how their tonsils were not sunburned.

Oddly, we have an innate need for friends but often deny this need on the grounds of time, insecurity, or pride. The devil laughs. He knows how vital Christian friends are for our path, and he will toss barriers before us to prevent what God wants for us. Frighteningly often, he succeeds, and we move on with our busy lives alone and worse for it.

Interestingly, the Bible even places friends above family at certain times of distress. Proverbs 27: 10 tells us, "Do not forsake your friend or a friend of your family, and do not go to your relative's house when disaster strikes you – better a neighbor nearby than a relative far away."

Big Bill

One memorable friend of mine came into my life when I was in my twenties, and he was in his sixties. A militant Alcoholics Anonymous twelve-step member, I will call him Big Bill because of his size and to honor Bill W., who founded AA and saved my friend's life. He taught me a great deal about people and something about the twelve-step programs. The saying that there is no saint like a reformed sinner could have been coined based on him and his life. One of his favorite sayings was, "Trust in the Lord and clean house." A cleaner house I have never seen.

He always emphasized how we were struggling human beings who can make ourselves stronger or weaker. He told me that by attempting self-control, he became weaker. Self-reliance, to him, was a liability. That still amazes me to this day. In admitting he was powerless over the bottle, he became stronger. In joining and assisting others in AA, he was able to crawl out of the dungeons of alcoholism and depression. In giving service and compassion to others, he received grace from the Holy Spirit that reversed his life. Big Bill made me realize that God's church is not built on people's strengths, but on God's ability to use people despite their failings, deficiencies, and sins.

He told me it was important to live life one day at a time. The future would come regardless. We have to take care of this day first. He helped me realize how important it is to have Christian friends on our life voyage to both learn from and to provide encouragement to on the path we have been given.

One somewhat puzzling thing he shared with me was that the twelve-step programs were not designed to open up the gates of heaven. Instead, they were meant to open up the gates of hell and give you the chance to get out. Not being a member, I will trust that he was right in his

77

observation and that he and countless others had escaped demon rum's grasp through this program borne of the Holy Spirit.

One thing he taught me was an acronym that was something like FHALT for Fearful, Hungry, Angry, Lonely, and Tired, each of which can cause one to "fall off the wagon." These feelings will occur frequently. No human can escape them. They are part of daily life. He emphasized that each person had to be vigilant to the degree that they are impacted by them. To each, it will be different, but behavioral disorders can occur when you have a FHALT.

He once told me a story that was instructive on how we, especially men, relate to each other. He said he was in an alcohol rehabilitation center for men. After being in the facility for a while, a man was given two slips of paper from each of the other men. The first slip contained a negative thing about them, the second a positive thing. They were then made to read the first slips in front of all of the men. They may have been belligerent, angry, or upset about what was written, but they read them. Then they read the second slips, the positive things others said about them. This was when they broke down and cried. They often felt they didn't deserve such good things to be said about them. As much as these kind words meant to them, imagine how much more God must love them and you. Possibly God's greatest miracle in our lives is that He loves us most when we are our most unlovable.

Happenstance

Your path may well run into others as arranged by the Holy Spirit with you chalking it up to happenstance. An overheard conversation can be vital to your understanding of a friendship. The attitude toward you one morning by your boss may impact your emotional state for the rest of the day. That new coworker, who now sits beside you, can influence your set routine. Brief, but influential, can best describe these casual encounters with the rest of the human race. Their immediate impact can be minimal or decisive on your daily path. These are often minor critical junctions and reflect a judgement of the Holy Spirit to impact your life.

Still, others may be placed in your life or, as you might say, "in my way," as you resent their incursion or welcome their impact. Regardless, your reactions toward them will be decided by you and their presence in your life by God.

Happenstances can be those things of importance and value.

Puzzle Pieces

Sit for a moment and consider the following questions. Look on them as a means to discover jigsaw puzzle pieces of your life and consider how they fit into your scheme of life. Your path was undoubtedly influenced by others, and the extent can be more or less measured in retrospect. Some influences may seem more prominent than others, but each has had an impact on the trajectory of your life.

- Were you the favorite child, just another one of the kids, or the "lost child" in your family? How did that affect both you and the family dynamics?
- What were some of the unwritten rules of your family when you were growing up, and how do they influence you to this day?
- If married, list two strengths and two weaknesses in your relationship. Will those be encountered in the coming week?
- If married or considering marriage, what mutual interests do you have with your partner?
- If you have children, there are probably 5,632 ways your life has changed because of them. What are two? What is coming down the pipe the coming year with them? Can you prepare in advance for them?
- Who were your two most influential teachers, and why were they important to you? How did they influence you?
- Who was your favorite minister, and why were they good for you? How did they influence you?
- Who were your favorite friends in grade school and high school? What were the friendships based upon?
- What types of friends do you seem to attract? Why is that?
- Did you ever have a mentor, and, if so, what life lessons did they teach you?

Dan Boozan

- Has anyone entered your life by happenstance, even just for a brief encounter, and had an impact on you? What was it?

6. Social Groups

Some of us are joiners, some of us abhor groups. Some of us thrive in a social milieu, some of us withdraw from such. Some cannot join enough clubs while others quote Groucho Marx in that, "I refuse to join any club that would have me as a member."

There are many social groups we may feel called to join. Some are permanent and well-established, such as scouting organizations or the Lions clubs. Some are transient, such as the office bowling team or a church's Financial Peace University classes.

According to the National Center for Charitable Statistics (McKeever, 2019), there are over one and a half million tax-exempt organizations involved in charitable work, food collection, transportation, teaching, etc. Further, over eight billion hours of service are annually volunteered in the United States with local scout troops, building Habitat for Humanity homes, distributing food to the needy, and serving as officers in a variety of clubs. Some, such as the American Legion, are national, while others, such as local recycling groups, are known only in their community.

In that Christianity is a way of life, we may be called by Him to serve in one or several capacities in such groups. From our church duties, to buying Christmas gifts for the Salvation Army's impoverished children, to weekend work at an animal rescue shelter, the opportunities are almost limitless. Some are strictly social, like the office darts team, some are to develop personal skills, such as Toastmaster's International, while others are for the community good, like the Optimists.

But what is your calling, if any, to these social groups?

Here we are examining the abundance of additional opportunities you may be called to serve in for your betterment, your neighborhood's betterment, or both. These can be for a set period of time or a lifelong involvement. Your skills may be well suited for or essentially non-existent for your social group's calling.

Virtually all involve interacting with your fellow man, a commitment of time, and, possibly, an outlay of money. Your ego may need to be checked at the door as you provide services to others. Your abilities may be strained to the limit as you spearhead new projects. Your heart may be bruised as your efforts go unnoticed or rebuked. Regardless, you may be called upon to walk down such trails of God's choosing.

We learn a little more about ourselves and the life path we are being called down by God when we realize the social groups we are attracted to. Direct service to the impoverished may be a personality indicator you never considered before as you serve meals at a homeless shelter. You may be called upon to develop gifts bestowed upon you, such as in public speaking in Toastmasters International. A calling to leadership can be explored and developed in the Rotary and other clubs. Your path may involve self-improvement groups or those that are strictly altruistic. Youth leadership can be gleaned in Boy and Girl Scout leadership roles. Person-to-person service can be given through the Alzheimer's Association and the National Ovarian Cancer Coalition. A natural proclivity toward religion can be used as you serve as a greeter or office manager at your local church.

We are given natural inclinations for a purpose. You don't find yourself in the fast lane of your abilities and interests to put on the brakes.

You will find that satan can find and exaggerate reasons to avoid such callings. Proverbs 22:13 speaks of excuses not to be involved, "The sluggard says, 'There is a lion outside! I'll be killed in the public square!'" Joining the Lion's club may seem distressing at first, but your life path may lead you to collect eyeglasses for them in the public square. Regardless, you will probably survive, but your sluggard ways may need to be killed to serve the Lord.

How do you feel you are being called upon to use and develop your traits, interests, and abilities? Possibilities are:

- Service to your church
- Service to your fellow man
- Leadership
- Community betterment
- Social justice
- National/World causes
- Personal improvement

Your answers will tell you more of God's plan for you and help you put pieces of your Life Puzzle together.

Churches

A church can be a nurturing place, teaching us how to grow in faith, knowledge, and grace from God. It can also be a place where egos collide over trivial matters, unimportant doctrine debates occur, and pride rears up. All can be provided and often are.

A church often cultivates a tranquil appearance, but rarely is that the reality. It is an intense place. Intense in faith, love, emotions, work, and beliefs. Lift the lid, and a beehive of activity is found, both obvious and not.

God's path will require you to profess your faith in a public way and one of the most important is church membership. Different Christian churches worship in different ways, with different beliefs, and different services. You can evolve into what Jesus wants you to be depending on your adherence and dedication to follow church doctrine, study the Bible, serve within your church, and accept critical junctions it will provide. Prayer, family and friends, and reflection on critical junctions regarding religion can guide you to a church or denomination if needed.

What you get out of this vital component of God's life for you will, in large part, be a reflection of your effort.

Friendships can spring up. Happiness can grow. Life can become fuller in satisfaction. Insights into your place in God's world can be gained. Families can be strengthened. Your children can be guided into lives you will be proud of. Comfort can be provided in times of illness or death.

Will you find it practical, easy, and painless to be member of a church? Of course not.

Yes, many positive outcomes can be yours and some were just listed, but Christianity never claimed to be practical, easy, or painless. Early church membership came with the promise of crucifixion. Later that became being fed to lions in the Colosseum. Today, adherents in other parts of the world are deeply discriminated against, even to the point of death.

The Los Angeles Times, in their disturbing article on Christmas, 2019, https://www.latimes.com/world-nation/story/2019-12-25/china-church-sinicization tells of the change in Christianity in China. At one time it was accepted, but in recent years "clergy are forced to change their sermons to align with 'socialist core values' and paste Communist Party slogans on the walls."

Chinese officials estimated in 2018 there were thirty-nine million adherents to Christ, with underground churches pushing that estimate up to eighty million. Today, Christianity is a guarantee of interrogation and possible prison sentences. The government is, as is noted in the article, revising the Bible and has established one "official" Christian church with sermons directed to enforce Chinese Communist Party leadership.

A horrifying *New York Times* article printed on December 27, 2019 https://www.nytimes.com/2019/12/27/world/africa/ISIS-executions-Nigeria.html described a video by the Islamic State in Nigeria where eleven Christians were slaughtered, ten by having their throats slashed. The voice-over said the killings were a "message for Christians."

I gave a dear friend and wonderful minister, Dan Hatfield, a t-shirt years ago that proclaimed "This shirt is illegal in 53 countries. Restricted nations: 40. Hostile areas: 13" because of the cross it displayed. That t-shirt can still be ordered, although I would not be surprised if the numbers have increased in more recent printings.

Even in Christian nations there are sneers and scorn to those who believe. There have been lawsuits in Arkansas for having a twelve commandments monument in public, against reciting the Lord's Prayer at city council meetings in Parkersburg, West Virginia, and an attempt that went to the Supreme Court to remove "In God We Trust" from currency.

Never doubt we belong to a church that persecution never ended for and will never until the second coming.

Today we live in a chaotic, dangerous, and frightened world. The wonderful pastor and author A.W. Tozer provided us with what Christian churches must become when he said, "A scared world needs a fearless church."

Your path will require church membership and the responsibilities so entailed. These are adult responsibilities and are needed to become a full adult in God's eyes. For a fearless church to impact a scared world it needs these adults. You will be doing it for your church family, your soul, and for a man who loved you two-thousand years ago.

Self-Improvement

There are many social groups that can help you improve who and what you are, as well as your community. The American Red Cross, ASPCA, friends of the library, Girl Scouts, local homeless shelters, Feeding America, and a thousand more are open and available.

You may feel a pull toward one of these groups, or have a critical junction guide you toward one. You may need to consider your strengths and your weaknesses for guidance.

On my personal trek I had a pulling toward one such group. I spent most of my life as a self-conscious, ill-spoken person, yet inside of me was a small yearning to become a competent public speaker. I knew that people were more afraid of speaking in front of large groups than of death and completely agreed with that assessment. My few public speaking occasions saw me so uptight you couldn't have pulled a needle out of my rear end with a bulldozer. No wonder my father used to tell me, "Keep your mouth shut every chance you get."

However, I admired eloquence in speakers and, upon learning of Toastmasters International, joined to develop tolerable speaking skills. Little did I suspect what the Holy Spirit had in mind for me.

That spark of interest and the encouragement of club members led me to find that I was able to write well for the ear. Words and phrases flowed well, speech structure improved over time, and my speeches became more robust and influential. My delivery method evolved from leaving death grip marks on the lectern, to being able to deliver my message up close and personal with my audience. I could articulate a vibrant message and won awards and accolades for my performances.

I have gotten over my fear of speaking in front of large groups, but have since noticed that large groups have developed a fear of me speaking in front of them. I'm certain that is just a coincidence.

The Lord gave me an interest in and a modicum of talent for public speaking. By His grace, I developed this small talent, which helped lead me to a future role as a trainer and presenter.

The Bible tells us of another who was ill-equipped to serve in this capacity. Moses apparently was poorly spoken, self-conscious, and felt unable to serve as a spokesperson for God's chosen people. Being raised in an Egyptian palace by a princess, his first language had to have been Egyptian, not the language of his people.

When called upon to lead the Israelites, he flat out refused and asked the Lord to inflict that task on Aaron. He wanted nothing to do with leadership or public speaking. Yet the Lord selected him for this commission and provided him with abilities he had not had up until they were needed.

Do not be surprised if you are given abilities you did not know you had in leadership, facilitation, public service, or other areas when you need them. These abilities may be temporary, but they are yours for a time and purpose. Still, other talents may be allotted to you for the balance of your life. It is what you do with these grants of grace that is vital. They may be conferred instantly, but more often, they may need to be developed under His tutelage. They are God's gifts to you, and you are meant to serve Him with them. Regardless, you will probably wonder where on earth you got a new ability from. It was not from earth.

Internet Groups

In this modern world, you can find websites that can pique your interest and give indications of what your path and purpose may be. There are interest groups available for virtually all human endeavors. From chess to shaving to model airplanes, there are internet sites and chat rooms available for you to explore.

This may well be the future of social groups, having a worldwide presence on the web for discrete topics, bordered only by the language used. Past that barrier, we can interact with others with enthusiasm and curiosity as we learn more on the set subject.

In this brave new world of the internet, we are granted anonymity if we so desire, and an open forum for our opinions and musings. However, the internet is a double-edged sword. Yes, we are interacting with others, but no, not directly. We lose the human connectivity we experience when face-to-face with our fellow man. Worse, it is far too easy to lie by presenting ourselves differently online than we could when working alongside another volunteer. Warmth and comradery are, to a degree, forfeited when working with others online. The web can serve as an important, and possibly necessary, adjunct to personal interaction, but cannot replace the human touch that seems to be an essential part of our DNA.

Temporary Service

Sometimes we will become involved with organizations on a temporary basis. My time with a professional organization lasted only as long as I worked as a programmer with a specific software. Similarly, you may work on a Habitat for Humanity house until completion or volunteer for a day at a local homeless shelter. My church adopted an impoverished family that I delivered meals and goods to for a year. These can be testing grounds for your temperament to a line of service and help you determine if you are being called to serve Him in a specific capacity. We may find we excel, or fail, in these brief tours of duty. Organizing a neighborhood yard sale may be ready-made for our interests, abilities, and the length of time we wish to invest. Yet through it, we may find puzzle pieces of personality that are vital to understanding ourselves.

Changes to Ourselves

His purposes may seem obscure to us as we work alongside others to recycle community waste or teach others the basics of reading. We may not realize what is truly happening until we recognize that we are not only providing services, support, and confidence to others, but simultaneously nourishing our personal needs. Often the Lord's goal for us is not only to help others, but to change us through our services to Him. We can develop friendships, build self-reliance, and make ourselves better in His eyes through our volunteer work. The change is as much inside as it is outside of ourselves.

I once spent a day serving in a community homeless shelter for men and, after my tasks were done, I sat down in the dining room to simply chat with those men. At first, they seemed hesitant to talk to me. I had the impression that other volunteers didn't bother to do so. One man wanted to talk, but seemed reluctant. He stammered on how his life was turning around and that he had been getting better. He seemed to want to let me know that he was going to be as good as he thought others outside of the shelter were.

I simply talked with him and the others about whatever they wanted. I treated them as I would anyone who I just met at work or church. That was what they seemed to want, that seemed to reassure them, and that was what they seemed to need. They just wanted someone who would accept them as they were, God's beloved people. I left after talking about two hours with them, but there was no question that my time conversing with them was the best service I could have given them. It helped and changed me a little bit, and it seemed to help them a little bit. We liked each other and respected each other. It was a small potion for their troubled souls and what God had planned for me to do all along.

Working with the Poor

Frequently, when we think of service organizations, we think of assisting the poor in our community. This is laudable and certainly a blessing to them, but the vice of pride can quickly corrupt our efforts. When working with the poor, we may soon find ourselves being judgmental and condescending. Our mindset may be the greatest determinant of how well we can serve His people.

Attitude is the key to success and pride the key to failure in such moments. It is easy to be judgmental toward the welfare family to whom we deliver food. We may disparage the homeless man who, after you fill his plate with food, tells you to add some more. A backbone of knowing you are serving our Lord and possessing an attitude that you will serve Him well can help mitigate the pride that can swell up inside us. It is pride that tries to slay our selfless efforts to serve others and has us compare ourselves to those others.

An attitude of gratitude and humility is necessary to serve. An attitude of gratitude may come easily as we are grateful for the blessings bestowed upon us. An attitude of humility, on the other hand, can conjure up images of being humiliated or groveling before others. In truth, being humble is based upon being modest, respectful, and knowing we do not know all. We must be taught by the Lord how to serve those whom His Son came to serve. Jesus came to serve the sick, the poor, and the sinners. We must do the same. We are the same.

The epitome of service to the poor could well be Mother Teresa, who served the utterly destitute in the slums of Calcutta. She never forgot that in serving them, she was serving God, who made those impoverished people in His image. It is instructive that she served a non-Christian people. It simply didn't matter to her. She saw God's face in each of them.

Puzzle Pieces

Your interests, personality, abilities, and weaknesses make up that unique person God has created called you. Consider these, then think of those organizations, formal and otherwise, that you may be called upon to serve Him through. Take time to reflect on things you have an interest in, such as writing, your church, or building things. There is probably a club or organization in your community that can benefit from you, and you can become enriched through participation in it.

List a minimum of three such organizations, with an emphasis on what you find yourself drawn toward regardless of your abilities. These may be strictly social, professional in nature, or service-oriented. But irrespective of their bent, list them as ideas on how God may be calling you.

After compiling your list, research the groups, possibly online, and write a short paragraph on each noting how they could benefit from you belonging to them, as well as how you could profit from them. Membership may follow in a day, a decade, or never, but you will be more attuned to how God is working within you, how He made you, and His path for you.

7. Education

From youth through young adulthood, education is a constant in our lives. Upon completing our formal education, we find employment, as best we are able, given the schooling we endured. Our education can, to varying degrees, define our employment and the rest of our lives.

Beginning in middle school, we are typically allowed to select courses and do so based on our interests, what we think will be easy, or that the cute person sitting next to us said they were going to take next year. Our experiences are good, bad, ambiguous, confusing, and erratic. We learn from our teachers and learn from our mistakes. We remember our mistakes longer.

At the end of high school, educational decisions are made for our immediate future, and, whether understood or not, we need guidance. Frequently, we will find ourselves influenced by others at this critical junction. Those placed in our lives at this time are often a compelling component of God's plan for us. Mentors, teachers, best friends, family, and even antagonists can all leave a decisive mark on our educational decisions. The Lord will guide us along His plan if we listen for Him and work to understand His will.

Educational Options

Formal education may well be needed to achieve your goals. College work may be required for your desired profession. Trade school and an apprenticeship may fit your gifts and personality well. The military may be your true calling when looking at your skills and interests. Regardless, the Lord has a plan for you, and the opportunity to serve Him will offered.

Your education is important to yourself, your family, and your future. You must serve as a good steward of it. Yet you must know that it will be Him who will define how it will impact your life. God will dictate how you and the education you receive will serve Him. Do not be surprised by surprises. A class that you take on a lark may well beckon you to a career. A passing interest in a field may lead to an advanced degree.

Further, you may well find yourself moving from your degree to an unrelated field once you begin your work life. With an aerospace engineering degree, your computer classes may cast you into a payroll programming job. As a business major, you may be called upon to serve a life as a pastor. A journalism major may find themselves overseeing a mutual fund transactions department. The Lord often seems to let us muddle through our educational lives and then places us on totally unfamiliar terrain. But it is where we are to serve Him.

It is important not to get caught up in the trap of thinking we must be a teacher, businessman, engineer, or programmer at all costs. In doing so, we may be placing that goal between God and ourselves. When anything comes between God and us, He may strike it down unmistakably. God loves us so much He does not want anything to stand between Him and us. An obsession with entering in one field may act to deny God's plan. We better serve Him when we follow what we feel is His path for us and say, "Above all, let Thy will be done."

Similarly, we cannot let short-sightedness rule our hearts and minds. I knew of a person who detested school so much they attended a trade school and studied to be a travel agent for no other reason than it took the least number of weeks of all programs offered. Later, when internet arrangements for travel became common, their small travel agency folded, and they were bereft of transferable skills. A long-range mindset that considers our interests, career hopes, personal limitations, and educational wants may serve us better and Him best.

For many, a continuous progression of structured, continuing education classes, as well as informal or online learning, may be the norm for life. Society and technology changes are relentlessly, and continued learning may well be on God's predefined path for you. We must trust in His guidance and, as noted, be able to say, "Above all, let Thy will be done."

Selecting Your Educational Path

So how are we to proceed with determining our education and, potentially, our life's work?

In the Interests section of this book, it was noted that if you want to find your true, innate interests, look at what you enjoyed doing as a child. What did you like to read on? Did you enjoy collecting things? Were you drawn to certain subjects? Did you build things, enjoy Scouts, design houses, or play with pets? By answering these questions, you can gain a better feel for what could lead to happiness in your studies and career. These could be pointers provided by God.

As discussed earlier, taking standard personality and career assessment tests can help you muddle through the confusion most of us experience in our teen years and early adulthood. These tests can help identify your most vital traits and interests, and the fields that thrive on people with your personal qualities.

You may be out of college but can still take such tests at local college placement centers or online. These can help guide you toward the degree and profession you may be best suited for, but never lose sight that you were meant to live a life, not just receive a degree. Your Life Mission statement and Plan of Action, to be done at the end of this book, can duly incorporate your findings, but obtaining a degree is but one facet of that spark of inspiration, vitality, and confidence in that grand mosaic that is you.

You were born with inherent, God-given talents, abilities, and interests. Your education can reflect them. Your work career goals can be based upon them. Your school life can be grounded on the passions God has placed in your heart.

When you love what you study, you will excel at it, and it will never seem to be a burden. God apportioned to you distinct abilities, passions, skills, talents, opportunities, and limitations. Using them in your life is using them for the Lord.

Yet, almost depressingly, we must also temper our educational aspirations by self-knowledge gleaned from our life experiences, our intellectual limits, and knowledge of the ways of the world. Having a poor mind for math does not a scientist make. A passion for the theater must consider the difficulty of finding employment in that field. The world cannot employ as many football coaches as there are people with that interest. The world speaks loudly, and we must ask the Lord to guide us through it. We must temper our passions with knowledge of the limits of the world and confines within ourselves. Alfred Adler counseled us well, "Follow your heart, but take your brain with you."

This is one of the hardest lessons we will ever learn, and, regrettably, we are forced to do so in our youth. We are required to choose our educational path, knowing we may not have our passions fully set upon it, but that it seems to be the way the Lord is calling us given our skill set. We can set sail to pursue a degree in a field that we indeed have an interest in and reasonable hopes of a career. Our educational decisions will be made, and we will pursue them to the best of our abilities. We may attend a university, enter the military, or leave for a trade school, but we must follow and fulfill what we feel is His path.

Formal Education

If we decide on a formal education, we are allowed to select from a large number of paths but must buffer our selection by knowing our intellectual limits and personality. We follow a degree or training path and spend our time, money, and dreams on it. We will undoubtedly find ourselves imagining a career that our education will catapult us into. We will also hear of others who dreamed the same and were left with only dreams and empty hands. Still, we will dream, attend classes, and study.

We learn time management, perseverance, dedication, and other life skills that may serve us better than our degree. Our classes will teach us the rudiments of our proposed career path, and we will feel we are ready to move mountains in that field. We often find that our confidence builds, our egos expand, and our potential for a reality check magnifies.

When you reach the formal conclusion of your education and are grasping that diploma, you are commonly greeted with bad news. You may find that your college degree only serves as a ticket into the work world. Your resume will be considered by employers before those without a degree. In a few fields, such as medicine and engineering, it will directly lead to the job you think you want. In other fields, your degree will have little bearing on your work and career path.

You may find that the diploma you spent blood, sweat, tears, and much money getting may not get you a job even remotely in your field. I feel all diplomas should come with a warning from the Surgeon General - *Warning! Acceptance of this sheepskin could be hazardous to your mind* (not to mention to the sheep's). We may have planned on a specific career, but we will find that it is God's will that will prevail.

Informal Education

As important as a formal education may seem, an informal education may be just as practical, if not more so. My time handling drunks at a late-night fast food restaurant taught me more about behavioral disorders than my minor in psychology ever did.

Learning discipline and responsibility from a job while attending college may be the most valuable education you can get. Handling your finances can be a valuable education unto itself. The friendships you make with your fellow students can be a source of opportunity, comfort, and comradery for a lifetime. An investment of time in extracurricular activities can blossom into skills, expertise, and contacts ready for use upon graduation. Understand that education can come from life as well as from classes.

As mentioned before, if you learn one good thing from every book you read, class you take, and person you spend much time with, you are way ahead of the game. Study well in your school years, but do not neglect the necessity of informal education.

In that informal education, you may find others placed in your life at critical junctions, whether you realize it or not, for your personal edification. A favorite work supervisor who encourages you, a fellow student who tells you what to avoid, or a strict boss who makes sure you perform quality work all can serve in this regard. They may be placed in your life for a set purpose. The lessons to be learned from them may be harsh but necessary. God made the world a harsh place. He knows you often learn best from adversity, and the world is ready-made to teach you lessons in responsibility, determination, and competency. Others may be serving God's purposes in your life by the leadership, comradery, and tasks they give you. You should approach the world aware of that.

The World

The world is the greatest provider of education, and we often receive a failing grade. The school of hard knocks will knock hard at our door, and we open it wide. We find we don't have the right kind of insurance for wind-blown rain damage to our house. Our health insurance is not right for our illness. The car has an electrical problem that we didn't know it could have. Our children ask how you say hula-hoop in Chinese. The list is endless, and we can find that problems beset us that we lack solutions to or even knew they could exist.

Yet we can attempt to learn from these and move onward with our lives. It is a wise person who continues their education deliberately and diligently. The Dave Ramsey Financial Peace University classes offered by many churches can be a Godsend of practical knowledge on personal finances. The internet is replete with trade groups providing advice such as the NAIC's insurance information. Libraries contain books on topics from cooking to auto repair to computers. Opportunities are available to you.

We can also ignore the teachings of the world as too much of a burden and bear the consequences. Legions have walked both paths. Attempt to learn when you can.

Puzzle Pieces

If you are looking at selecting a college major then, as mentioned in the section on personality traits, interests, and abilities, it is recommended that you take personality and interest assessment tests designed to guide you toward an education and career. These can be found at local community colleges by contacting staff guidance counselors, as well as at some high school counseling offices. Many such tests are now provided online. Alternately, you can use the listing of traits and interests in that section to help guide you.

After reviewing the results, note your strengths as well as weaknesses. Consider and review the educational options available. Tune into the interests you have, then pray and ask trusted family, friends, teachers, and mentors for their advice. Finally, notice how your heart is being drawn, pray some more, and decide on a direction for your education.

Now, regardless of your life situation, write a half-page essay on the educational path you are being drawn toward and, most importantly, why.

What do you need to learn today and throughout your life?

What does God want you to learn over the next year?

Is God calling you to serve Him in a specific capacity? Will you put in the time and effort needed for your educational path? How does He need you to attend to His people with your talents and abilities?

8. Work

Education followed by a career is the life sequence most of us go through. We complete our formal education, find employment, and then sink or swim in the job we have obtained. Some of us go through this effortlessly, yet many times we sink, and for reasons we may not understand at the time. Our personality is not suited for the position; we don't understand why we are doing what we are charged with; we clash with those in authority; we are given too much of a workload initially, etc. So, we sink and try other jobs and often other work fields. We pay our dues and our educational loans with significant interest on both.

Your college degree may directly lead to the job you think you want. More frequently, your career path will resemble the convoluted route on the Candyland game board, complete with a double order of cherry pits.

Colleges, in particular, focus on preparing their charges for a lifelong career in a select field. Yet how many of us are in professions that have no relationship to our college degrees? Our names are Legion. This disconnect seems so common as to be the rule.

Your degree may not even relate to the jobs you will spend your life in. The plural, jobs, is accurate in that it is a rare individual who spends forty-one years on the same job for the same company as my father did. Today, we expect to move between different companies and are usually not disappointed.

There are notable exceptions in fields such as engineering, law, and medicine where the degree and the profession are duly linked. But some occupations seem to thrive on hiring those with little background in their field. One of my better supervisors oversaw the transactions department of a mutual fund company, yet held a degree in journalism. The same for a bank accountant I knew. A good friend of mine in college obtained a degree in Recreation and now handles computer hardware. My first computer supervisor had his master's degree in ichthyology (the study of fish). A friend of a friend received a law degree at an ivy league university, but after a year in practice jettisoned that for a career as a hedge fund manager. My degrees in Public Administration and Computer Science provide some benefit to my software training and documentation career but are far from ideal.

We indeed plan, but it is the Lord's will that will prevail, not our college degree.

Our Work Path

Once settled into a job, we hopefully will enjoy its work. Ecclesiastes 3:22 states, "So I saw that there is nothing better for a person than to enjoy their work because that is their lot. For who can bring them to see what will happen after them?" We often don't know what will happen in our careers, or, for that matter, what will happen each workday. Regardless, we find our work paths, quite possibly in unforeseen ways.

You may be called to work, or even lead, in a position your education is utterly destitute in. It is possible the Lord made you to serve as a Christian example to others in such a position. It is also possible you want nothing to do with such a position. What may seem surprising is that God frequently has those not well-suited, skilled, or willing to lead a ministry for Him. Moses and Jonah were examples in the Old Testament. The alcoholic Bill W. founded Alcoholics Anonymous. The slave ship captain, John Newton, who wrote "Amazing Grace," led the fight against slavery in England.

It can be argued that Moses' path toward leadership started when he murdered an Egyptian. Later he told God to choose Aaron, not him, for the leadership of His chosen people. Yet it was Moses who led his people to the Promised Land. God, without question, works in mysterious ways.

Should we be concerned if our background and skills are not what is needed for a position? Should we be worried if we seem called upon to serve as a Christian work example? What if we are convinced that we are not suited for such a calling? One such example came during the last century. C.S. Lewis' journey began as he attempted to disprove Christianity and ended with him being one of the most influential Christian writers of that century. He might well have declared himself unworthy to serve as an example of Christianity as a way of life, yet his legacy as such lives on to today.

When we are feeling called or are simply thrust into such a position, we must pray, rely on the Holy Spirit, and work with others. Guidance will come, and abilities may be enabled. St. Augustine, who is quoted as saying, "God grant me chastity, but not yet," began as a devout pagan who later championed Christianity at a critical point in its development. That there is no saint like a reformed sinner was evidenced by his installation as a bishop after his many affairs and an illegitimate son. Similarly, the noted theologian Dorothy Sayers was an adulteress who bore a child out of wedlock.

We can even see the guidance of the Holy Spirit in clearly non-Christianity related situations. The murderess Jean Harris reconstituted herself to become a champion of incarcerated women and their children.

They were called, and they answered as best they were able in spite of their failings. The Lord often uses those who have fallen far to lead His ministries. We must know that He will lead us if we allow Him to.

Christianity at Work

A minister friend told our congregation the story of a businessman he knew some years back. They had concocted a scheme where they would call people and sell them worthless investments. Until they were caught. The man was at that time awaiting sentencing in court.

The businessman asked the minister why God was allowing this to happen to him. My friend asked him if, at any time, he had asked for God's guidance, involvement, and blessing on his business. Of course, the answer was no. His supposed Christianity had been checked at the door when he went into his office to scam others.

We also can easily find our Christianity checked at the door when we look at the role of work in our lives. It may never occur to us that we are to be Christians in the workplace, not workers in the workplace and Christians outside of the workplace. Christianity was not meant to be checked at the door. By our attitudes, behaviors, and actions, we are examples for coworkers of Christianity as a way of life. This may be one of the most significant parts of God's path for us.

Instead of considering our work time as a component of an overall Christian life, we often find our work becoming our primary focus in life with Christianity finishing a poor second in the race. We spend roughly a third of our lives asleep and a third of our lives at work, worrying about work, or on our commutes to work. The remaining third is all that is left for our overburdened lives. Yet our sleep and free time are often affected by our preoccupations with work. Being able to disengage our lives from our work is difficult for many of us.

C.S. Lewis noted in his book *The Great Divorce* that we often end up saying, "I now see that I spent most of my life in doing neither what I ought nor what I liked." Often it seems our work lives are neither what we ought nor what we like and obsess upon them we do. As obvious as it is, it may never sink in that work is simply a component of a Christian life.

So how are we to handle this third of our lives? A Christ-centered work life most certainly is what He envisions for each of us. Ecclesiastes 5:18-20 tells us, "This is what I have observed to be good: that it is appropriate for a person to eat, to drink, and to find satisfaction in their toilsome labor under the sun during the few days of life God has given them – for this is their lot. Moreover, when God gives someone wealth and possessions, and the ability to enjoy them, to accept their lot and be happy in their toil – this is a gift of God. They seldom reflect on the days of their life, because God keeps them occupied with gladness of heart."

We may well find that our "satisfaction in their toilsome labor under the sun" is based upon His calling for us to serve as an example to others of a Christian-based work life. Our service and example to others is what is paramount in His eyes. The actual work is of minor importance. In that work, do not expect to be called to move mountains. As a rule, we are meant to move foothills, and, in doing so with a Christian demeanor, the mountains will know of it.

So how do we do our work in a Christ-centered way? By imitating our Lord in our dealings with others and performing quality work as we are able. These will honor and serve Him. Our attitude, thoughtfulness, respect, and warmth toward our fellow man will be noted by Him whom we will be serving and, possibly, even by our fellow man as well.

The Hebrew word "avodah" well represents how our labor serves to worship Him. It is simultaneously defined as work, worship, and service. In it, we find a route of serving through our labor. Colossians 3:23-24 implores us, "Whatever you do, work at it with all your heart, as working for the Lord, not for human masters, since you know that you will receive an inheritance from the Lord as a reward. It is the Lord Christ you are serving."

We need to understand that our avodah is not just our nine to five drudgery, but is however and whenever we serve Him through serving others. Mary, the mother of Jesus, did not hold an office job; her avodah was raising our Lord. We need to realize that our avodah is living out our work, as well as daily lives, moment by moment as Christians.

How we are to live our work lives may also be seen in Philippians 2:14-15, "Do everything without grumbling or arguing, so that you may become blameless and pure, 'Children of God without fault in a warped and crooked generation.'" Here we are instructed on how to respond to unreasonable demands, irritated customers, and inept managers. In doing so, we serve Him and demonstrate to others the power of Christianity as our way of life. It is worth noting that a "warped and crooked generation" is not relegated to that generation two thousand years ago.

One encouraging effort toward Christianity being practiced in the workplace is the advent of Christian breakfast meetings, work prayer groups, and after-hours fellowship gatherings. These can provide workers with encouragement, guidance, and support to proclaim the good news of Jesus Christ at their jobs through their actions and words. Members become empowered to serve God and follow in the footsteps of His Son, Jesus Christ.

Work Situations You May Face

You will find many challenging work situations in all jobs. The good, the bad, the ugly, and even the beautiful can all appear and often in the same week.

U.S. Park Ranger Roy Sullivan holds the world record for being hit by lightning seven times and surviving each strike. You may find yourself envying him as you find yourself a lightning rod for customer complaints as you work your first job in retail, fast food, or customer service. Seven strikes or more in a day may be your initiation to the working world.

103

You may be annoyed, aggravated, and exasperated in your employment. You may find your job is an irritable bowel syndrome gone off the chart. You can see your daily tasks as "challenging opportunities" as one of my employers phrased it or as roughage for your system as we employees viewed it. Possibly, if things are that bad, you may have been put there to make them better and serve as an example to others. Possibly you are in the right field, but the wrong job. Possibly, and maybe painfully, you may need to move on. Prayer and consultation with trusted others can help guide you on the path you need to follow. A truism is that people do not quit companies; they quit management. Your manager and the management of your company, good or bad, may well be the most important factor in determining whether you decide to stay or leave.

Some organizations we enter seem fine from the outside but are as big as life and twice as ugly on the inside. They thrive on chaos and mismanagement. In those settings, your competency and calmness might serve as a blessing and beacon to those around you. In such a dysfunctional organization, you might be in the position of being the best-looking horse in the glue factory. But you will be the best and others may well notice.

Still, other jobs help you understand why the word customer begins with "cus." I was disheartened when my step-daughter announced that she was refusing to work Sunday afternoons as a hostess at her restaurant. The patrons who came in after church services were often belligerent, irritable, and unreasonable — a poor showing by our side. Prayers, tolerance, and providing a Christian example may be all you can offer as you serve your fellow man.

What if you find yourself the office squeaky wheel? You might harbor the elements of needed change that can begin by your squeaks. However, a cautious path will need to be tread. In many organizations, the squeaky wheel is what gets replaced.

Then again, you may be the ideal worker whose job gets the axe because of mistakes made by managers you didn't know existed. Similarly, you may lose your job owing to work failures of others a thousand miles away, a general layoff because of a drop in the company stock price, or personality conflicts between the VP over your department and the CEO. Losing a job can be a body blow to your heart, finances, and dreams. Yet, even at its worst, God in the prayer "I Am

There" (discussed later) has told us He will be there throughout this period of your life. The word "restore" begins with "rest," and His means of restoring you to His path may well start with such a rest. You will meet others who also lost their jobs at one point or another, and they will be known to you as Legion. Regardless, He will be there, and your path will continue.

On the positive side, you may find an expression of grace in the form of a mentor at work. As discussed earlier, often, these are the oldest and most experienced workers. They know all the shortcuts that you don't. They are seeing retirement on their horizon and may want to leave a legacy at work by serving as an unofficial advisor to you. Their help and encouragement, as well as their warnings and rebukes, can be invaluable.

A college professor of mine served as something of a mentor to me. In my Intro to Computer Science class, he admonished a number of us saying we were doing things the hard way and that the lazier you are, the better you will do in this field. After class, I told him I was going for my Ph.D. His lesson on finding easier means to accomplish work still resonates with me to this day in the adage, "Work smarter, not harder."

Other advice came from my Intro to Business professor, who told me that the first thing you do at work is to make yourself invaluable. Still, another professor helped me get a job one summer as a pea picker migrant worker. I learned the meaning of the words "culture shock" and became a better person for having gone through it. By the end of the summer, I even forgave him.

Special Roles

Occasionally, situations may arise that allow you to serve at work in a special role or capacity.

Projects, often poorly defined, may be thrust upon you with "Do good and avoid bad" being the only marching orders given. Trust in the Lord, seek His inspiration, pray for guidance, and then work like a dog. His inspiration may come in the form of necessity bordering on desperation and fueled by exhaustion. As one wag best put it, "Inspiration is that thing you go after with a club." But He will be there if you involve Him from the beginning. Regardless, you are ultimately serving Him as you progress through the project and serve as an example to others.

105

At other times, you may find yourself needing to make a significant decision for the organization. The choices may be as obvious as building a better mousetrap or building a worse mouse, but many will back building a worse mouse. Your decision will be as much based on your convictions as your growing business knowledge. First, pray, then speak with others, then trust in God and act.

Still again, you may face situations where others will come out of the woodwork offering to do your work for you. This may be the best solution, or you might learn the quote, "There is no free lunch, but for the rest of your life, someone will offer you one." Regardless, you will know them by the commissions they will be making off you. These may be good investments or bad choices. Prayer, reflection, and knowledgeable others can guide you.

At times, you may be called upon to become an expert in a field. So, what is an expert? I once read that an expert is anyone who has read two books on a subject, simply because most of us refuse to read more than one book on a subject. Your calling may be to serve as an expert in a highly specialized capacity for your business. The path you may find you have trod to become such an expert may not be obvious until you have reached such a summit.

It is always possible that you will have that unique, innate blend of characteristics that will set you apart in the work world. The Lord may have blessed you with the temperament, abilities, skills, and interests ideally needed for a highly specialized job. Then again, you may be in a unique situation whether you want to or not. The Pony Express, the mail service through Indian territory in the 1860s, when advertising for riders, used to specify "orphans preferred."

Your work path may find you drinking deeply from one specific place at the fountain of knowledge or simply walking around it and gargling and spitting a lot. Generalists also have their place of toilsome labor under the sun. A well-rounded education and disjointed career path may be perfect for the temperament, qualities, and spirit you were given. It can take a great deal of skill to serve in a general capacity. Ministers, in particular, are noteworthy in this regard as they work with theology, finances, counseling, youth leadership, music, and more.

As a specialist, decision-maker, generalist, or in another role, you can define your means to serve the Lord. Consider keeping an up-to-date list of your experiences and accomplishments for work purposes, resume possibilities, and to help you better see the path you have plotted in the work world. By tracing your past, you can better gauge your future. Possibly your future path will become clearer as you note your past, the skills you gained, experiences you had, and the people you worked with. Retrospect can show you where life's puzzle pieces were added on His intended path for you.

Along our way, it is essential to celebrate and enjoy the work life we are given. Ecclesiastes 8:15 tells us, "So I commend the enjoyment of life, because there is nothing better for a person under the sun than to eat and drink and be glad. Then joy will accompany them in their toil all the days of the life God has given them under the sun."

We will undoubtedly toil during our days under the sun, but it will be our attitude that determines if we have joy accompanying the work we do.

New Talents

You may take count of your God-given talents today as you consider your life's work, but know that He may bestow additional gifts as your life progresses. At critical junctions in your life, you may find you are given abilities you didn't have until His selected moment.

As noted, Moses was ill-equipped for command until a critical junction came in his life. Grace was bestowed upon him as a speaker and leader, and with those tools, he led His people out of Egypt.

Do not be surprised if you find that you are given abilities at times and wonder how you got them. It may be instantaneous, but most likely, you will be given an interest, then a talent, and then the means to develop that talent through your efforts. There will be initial failings, but eventually opportunities to serve our Lord using it. Grace can be bestowed, and often is, in our careers.

Then again, you may be thrown in over your head and be given the needed talent to swim on the spot.

One thing to note is that we may not recognize God's grace being bestowed on us. Often it looks like something we deserve. Promotions, accolades, and opportunities may be given that we never expected, or we may have felt are well overdue. Still, He will decide to provide them to us and they may herald an opportunity to serve Him as a Christian example at our work. 1 Samuel 2:30 guides us, "Those who honor Me I will honor." What we do with this unmerited favor is vital and will testify to our character and service toward God.

Critical Junctions at Work

Your career path may be based on excellent advice, unquestionable abilities, a keen interest in a field, and a hunger to work in a specific career. Or it might be based on an odd coincidence or awful advice you were given and later recognize as a critical junction.

I knew a retired Air Force colonel who was told that those who signed up for air traffic controller school were to be let out of basic training a week early. He had never considered such a duty, but wanted out of basic training so badly that he signed up. Instead, he was in his hated basic training an additional week because of a delay. Yet he fulfilled thirty years in a duty he dearly loved.

At work, we may find others and situations placed in our lives at critical junctions, regardless of whether we realize it at the time or not. A coworker who teaches us a new skill, a project that helps us understand processes better, or a transfer to a position that is a better fit for our abilities and temperament all can serve as critical junctions. All can be a blessing from the Holy Spirit.

My current job came from an unknown source as I was called and offered an interview with a firm I didn't know existed. An improbable string of coincidences occurred that placed my name at the top of a recruiter's list. Once again, the Holy Spirit tapped me to serve in a new way.

Work and Your Life Path

Our work path is an important facet of what we are, but only a facet. Men, in particular, may find that this one facet of our lives distorts what we are being called to do with those lives. We may find that we like and are good at our work, but that it is an ill fit for our overall lives in terms of time taken from our family, the demands for production, the insecurity of knowing we may be terminated to satisfy the bottom line, or the high-pressure atmosphere. Work often places blinders on our will and even common sense. It can be disruptive to our Christian path, but can also be a calling to bear up and serve our fellow man as Christian examples.

The work world is ready-made to derail many of us from our Christian paths. Egos collide, failures abound, personalities clash, and pressures build. To be a Christian in this milieu will take all the nerve, strength, and mental ability you can muster. Yet we cannot set aside our Christian way of life to serve the company's bottom line. In fact, we must embrace the path we are given all the more. We must be prepared for graduate-level work in the school of hard knocks.

We must also know that jobs are a bit like computers. Every smart person has a backup. You may need to consider options and backups for your chosen profession. You should try to see your work future and navigate toward it through assignments, continuing education, caffeine, and dumb luck. But be aware of the influence of the Holy Spirit and critical junctions that may change your trajectory.

A Chinese proverb may be useful, "When the wind changes, some people build walls, some people build windmills." Developing windmill building skills while continuing your current daily tasks may bring blessings upon you and your family when you need them the most. In our modern world and with modern technology the wind continuously changes.

In the final analysis, we must bow before God and His work calling for us. We can be responsible and well-prepared workers in our careers. We can serve as models of Christianity as a way of life in our workplace. We may find that it is the Lord's plan to have stability in our careers, or we may find that we are to move to unrelated fields. Regardless, He makes His plans, and we are obliged to follow His call.

Puzzle Pieces

If you are considering deciding upon a career or changing your current job, then, as mentioned in the section on personality traits, interests, and abilities, it is recommended that you take personality and interest assessment tests designed to guide you toward an education and career. These can be found at local community colleges by contacting staff guidance counselors, as well as at some high school counseling offices.

109

Many such tests are now provided online. Alternately, you can use the listing of traits and interests in that section to help guide you.

After reviewing the results, note your strengths as well as weaknesses. Consider and review professions these are best suited and ill-suited for. Tune into the interests you have, then pray and ask trusted family, friends, teachers, and mentors for their advice. Finally, notice how your heart is being drawn, pray some more, and decide on a direction for your work life.

An invaluable resource can be the *What Color is your Parachute* book with a wealth of information on helping you decide on your work future.

If you are being drawn toward a different career than the one you are currently in, prayer may be intensely needed. How changing careers will impact your family and life must be part of your equation. A gradual moving may be possible, or serving the Lord by remaining in your current job may be decided upon. Regardless, serving Him is your goal.

Now, write a half page essay on the work path you feel drawn toward and, most importantly, why. Is God calling you to serve Him in a specific capacity? Will you put in the time and effort needed for this vocation? How does He need you to attend to His people with your talents and abilities?

9. Finances

Finances can be a fearful topic. People will tell you their sexual orientation before they tell you their annual salary. They may take you out and pay for the meal, then swipe the tip away from the waitress as they leave. Money can warp people's morals, behaviors, ways of thinking, and priorities.

Pride and fear seem anchored to our financial mindset. Proverbs 13:7 is instructive, "One person pretends to be rich, yet has nothing; another pretends to be poor, yet has great wealth."

Our path necessitates being good guardians of our finances, and that is among our hardest tasks. The puzzle piece that is money can be placed into many parts of our Life Puzzle, but only one is correct.

Some of us are afraid of being labeled Scrooges if we are frugal with our money. I have been quoted as saying that Scrooge was a very misunderstood man. A hard-working, dedicated capitalist, Scrooge exemplifies the worst aspects of capitalism that have made our country so great.

Yes, I go overboard on my praise of Scrooge, but my joke was to make a point. A frugal mindset may well be something to be praised.

We talk about the psychology of money on investment shows. The dollar can be financially healthy, strong, well, weak, or even sick. It may "want" to rise to a higher exchange rate or "feel itself" slipping against gold. Apparently, those greenbacks need psychotherapy, and the average Joe ends up paying the doctor bills.

Money, in and of itself, is a neutral object we use for our transactions. The problem with money, and what can make it so sinister, is how it perverts our personalities and affects our life's path. The man who would never dream of taking the last cookie from a tray could easily be the first to sign on to a shady business practice that promises a hefty profit margin. Proverbs 28:6 leads us with, "Better the poor whose walk is blameless than the rich whose ways are perverse."

Financial insolvency, perceived or real, can scuttle many of our hopes and plans. Being in debt can raise emotions ranging from concern, to worry, to terror. We will deny our situation, justify it, or simply sink into a depression and endure anxiety attacks with each creditor's call, but rarely are we indifferent to our plight.

Nothing seems to twist our values as much as cash. As of this writing, three individuals are splitting a one-point-five billion-dollar Powerball jackpot. If any of the three winners are single women, please feel free to interpret this book as a marriage proposal by your author. My wife has let it be known that she will tender the same offer if any of the three are single men.

The richest woman in America at one time, miser Hetty Green, allowed her son, whose leg was injured in an accident, to become so ill that it had to be amputated because she wouldn't pay for a doctor to treat it. She also used old newspapers collected from trash baskets in Central Park for undergarments. (Fowler, 1975)

The Bible speaks to money and wealth in many places, but nowhere as clearly as in 1 Timothy 6:10, where we are told, "For the love of money is a root of all kinds of evil. Some people, eager for money, have wandered from the faith and pierced themselves with many griefs."

Judas betrayed Jesus for thirty silver pieces. What he had planned to do with the money we will never know, but some think he bargained with the Pharisees to get as much as he could for our Lord's life. Today, we can easily find ourselves bargaining with our Lord to get out of our duty to tithe. The consequences may seem so minor in comparison, yet we must reflect on why we even feel the need to begin bargaining with God. We are in no position to bargain. Our sins are the reason His son was placed on the cross. He paid the full price for us; we are in His debt.

Money lust typically comes with two types of pressure, and they are from opposite ends of the financial spectrum. We are pressed to make it and then pressed to pay off what we have spent it on. Our personal financial statement has two bottom lines, one for what we have earned and one for what we owe. Rarely do they balance. You will find that satan knows well that greed and pride can rake havoc on our souls and lives when money is interjected into the equation.

We seem in competition not just to earn money, but to earn more money than our coworkers, our brother-in-law, or our spouse's father. Then comes the down payments for that newer motorcycle, house remodeling, or obligatory Disney World vacation. From them, the pressure builds for more income leading to more down payments.

The tail will simply not stop wagging the dog.

Ecclesiastes 5:10 puts it best, "Whoever loves money never has enough; whoever loves wealth is never satisfied with their income. This, too, is meaningless."

Friendships may be dropped, family ties severed, and church obligations ignored, but we will spend the time needed to make the cash necessary for our minimum VISA payments and to purchase the latest required toy.

If you want to know what God thinks of money, look at who He has given riches to. We may judge these to be fair and deserving or a pure waste of resources. Some did nothing more than be born into the right family, while others worked their fingers to the bone, and still others were smiled on by fortune with a fortune.

F. Scott Fitzgerald once said that the rich are different than you or me and, knowing only one side of that equation, I will assume he was correct. The rich can well be different in their aptitudes, talents, imaginations, and ability to see the future. A great strength of our nation is how the Horatio Alger's have climbed from their lowly starting points to make great successes of themselves to the benefit of society, as well as to themselves. They are to be admired for their courage, drive, and determination.

But at this rarified level the multi-billionaires reside on, deep concerns eat away at them as well. No amount of money can prevent fear; indeed, it can prod fear deeper. A number of recent news articles tell of their designing and building survival bunkers for a possible future apocalypse. One such article, in the *New Yorker* https://www.newyorker.com/magazine/2017/01/30/doomsday-prep-for-the-super-rich tells of private Facebook groups where the incredibly wealthy swap tips on gas masks, bunkers, and locations to hide. One member, the head of an investment firm, was quoted, "I keep a helicopter gassed up all the time, and I have an underground bunker with an air-filtration system." He said that his preparations probably put him at the "extreme" end among his peers. But he added, "A lot of my friends do the guns and the motorcycles and the gold coins. That's not too rare anymore."

The geographic remoteness of New Zealand is now being seen as its supreme advantage and many billionaires have built fortresses to withstand an electromagnetic, nuclear, biological or other type of future war https://www.bloomberg.com/features/2018-rich-new-zealand-doomsday-preppers/. Other locations hold these testaments to fear among the multi-billionaires. A fascinating Forbes magazine article provides proof of paranoia at this level https://www.forbes.com/sites/everbridge/2019/12/16/peace-of-mind-in-a-risky-world/#ffc328669c24.

It is telling that a private consultant to some of the wealthiest men in the world said, in an interview a few years ago, that one of the first questions the ultra-rich asked him was if they could trust their bodyguards if a cataclysmic event occurred. Would their bodyguards spirit him and his family to safety, or would they abandon him and save themselves and their loved ones instead?

Even those who have a personal wealth greater than the GNP of small nations live in fear. Many live lives chasing the almighty dollar, but disregard the Almighty.

The point is not how much money you make, but how it affects your character, behavior, morals, and priorities. You are called upon to be a good overseer of your life, and that would include your finances. The Lord will grant you opportunities to make money in your life, and your responses to these opportunities need to reflect Christianity as your way of life.

Money and Society

That our society is a financial addict can be seen by the rise and fall of the housing bubble in the recent past. People were told that they were entitled to the house of their dreams with no down payment. Then the bubble burst and splattered over our society for years. A home I purchased was a repossession from that time.

Societal pressures to make money can be subtle or brutal. Your spouse may want the finer things in life, your children may be influenced by their friends for toys of all types, and your employer may even expect you to have a certain lifestyle befitting their company image. You will face societal pressures to keep up expected appearances and buy those goods those in your socio-economic group are expected to have. Those pressures may warp your attitudes and priorities as readily as pressure warps wood. One of my all-time favorite cartoons is of the hapless character Ziggy. He was on the shore holding a fishing pole with the line leading into the ocean. Just further down was another line, but this was coming from the water on to the shore with a dollar bill attached to the hook.

TV and movies promote those goods we must have not only in commercials, but through prominent product placements in the center of the screen. Not only are they there, but they need to be in our homes as well. What's more, we feel entitled to have our next few years forfeited to pay these items off.

Fortunately, we can rely on the eventual help of those lottery tickets we buy with our fifth credit card. But what really happens with these lottery winners? Those fortunate few have left a disturbing legacy. *The New York Daily News* had an article, "Curse of the lottery: Tragic stories of big jackpot winners," (Bitette, 2016)) (Update https://www.nydailynews.com/life-style/tragic-stories-lottery-winners-article-1.2492941) which reported that nearly seventy percent of lottery winners end up broke within seven years. Further, several winners died tragically or saw those close to them suffer. The article detailed how bankruptcy, alcoholism, drug overdoses, and murder haunted those who won millions, with most ending up paupers.

Maybe lottery winnings should come with a warning from Ecclesiastes 6:2, "God gives some people wealth, possessions, and honor so that they lack nothing their hearts desire, but God does not grant them the ability to enjoy them, and strangers enjoy them instead. This is meaningless, a grievous evil."

It is telling that we celebrate the purchase of a thirty-year money pit mortgage, but never celebrate paying off the refrigerator. The new car, complete with a convenient seven-year loan, is bought with much fanfare, but we don't even notice that the trip to Hawaii only took two years to be paid off.

Dan Boozan

A wonderful pastor friend of mine told me that nothing will destroy a church faster than financial instability or immorality in the pulpit. Churches can go bankrupt, major organizations can fail, businesses can go under, and, of course, there is the wonderful example of the federal government's deficit.

Society is very much a financial addict, with financial slavery being considered the norm. Proverbs 22:7 tells us, "The rich rules over the poor, and the borrower is the slave of the lender."

In my Intro to Economics 101 class, we were taught that money flows to its most important usage. Apparently, among its most important uses are athlete endorsed tennis shoes, singer endorsed soft drinks, and actor endorsed VISA cards. Further, we are told that money will trickle down to the lowest economic groups. More commonly, those groups feel they are being trickled upon.

Interestingly, up until recently, some societies required purchasing goods with cash up front. The old Soviet Union required cash on the barrelhead from its citizens for items. But even it changed. One wag, when told that Soviet citizens could now buy items using installment plans, quipped that their enslavement was now complete.

The book, *The Best Encore,* provides us with the best explanation of the state of the American economy. The heiress and kidnap victim turned bank robber, Patty Hurst, was arrested and placed in jail awaiting trial. One of the earliest pieces of mail she received in her cell was an application for a credit card (Passell, 1977). When kidnapped, she apparently left home without it.

Money's Effects on Us

Money is a daily requirement on our path and, used correctly, is a minor blessing. Misused it can become an evil in our lives. Once again, the issue is not money itself, but how it affects us.

Debt can actually be seen as the drug of choice for some, with overdosing a common occurrence. We plunge into debt then buoy up to catch our breath before the next undertow drags us beneath again. As we feel the drowning sensation, a panic can set in that leads to fear, denial, and dread as we blame our family, bank, or Madison Avenue for our plight. Fear of opening letters from creditors becomes a way of life.

The number one cause of divorce in the United States is financial problems, and that statistic will probably not change. Bickering on what should be done with limited money can often be entered as a recurring event on our phone calendars.

Many years ago, I knew a woman who was clearly powerless over her spending. She and the man she was living with were told by their lawyer that if they stopped all spending immediately, there was a small chance they could avoid bankruptcy. A few days later, she went to one of her favorite antique stores and purchased a nine-hundred-dollar antique mirror. She was practically bawling explaining how good of a price it was, how it was worth so much more than that amount, and how it was truly an antique from France. I lost track of her after that, but never doubted her fate.

I've always held that couples considering living together should be required to get a joint checking account instead. If they are still talking to each other six months later, then one of them needs to propose marriage.

How we handle financial stress may very well determine the outcome of our marriage, our employment, how well we sleep, emotional ailments, happiness, and our children's welfare. It is a touchstone that will permeate much of our lives. It is to be handled with concern and respect.

Proverbs 13:8 tellingly starts with a warning, "A person's riches may ransom their life."

How many of us hold on to a job we detest for the money it brings in? We get caught in debt, so we are forced to stay in a job we hate to pay the bills. And along with paying the bills, we end up with ulcers, migraine headaches, and psychosomatic ailments. If we are honest with ourselves, we might realize that the equation boils down to simply wanting a lifestyle to show off to our friends and family, not how we actually want to live.

The deadly sin, greed, now comes to us in the guise of what we feel we deserve and what is best for our family. With it comes fear, anger, resentment, and pride. You will find that vices are often bundled together like a cell phone/TV/internet package, inseparable in effect. The tough love of denying our families what we want for them seems mean spirited and callous, but it can be necessary. Other families have the latest

117

creature comforts, shouldn't mine? My family deserves the best electronic gizmos a down payment can buy. Why not splurge, its only monthly payments? Greed comes ready-made with a thousand excuses; responsibility needs none.

Denying ourselves may even be harder. Many years ago, a fellow college student told me that he had just spent over a thousand dollars on computer equipment for himself, which he admitted were electronic toys. In his next breath he said that his family wasn't going to have much of a Christmas, the money just wasn't there for his three girls and his wife. The irony was utterly lost on him, but probably not his family.

Vices are often directly tied to our wallets. Judgment can go out the window after that third beer. Vegas offers free drinks to the players of one-armed bandits, and it is a sound investment on their part. Adultery can be an expensive habit, as well as gluttony and greed. Then there is gambling, which is in a league by itself.

In Ecclesiastes 2:10, Solomon said he had it all, but still, he wasn't content, "I denied myself nothing my eyes desired; I refused my heart no pleasure." Yet the next verse tells us, "everything was meaningless, a chasing after the wind; nothing was gained under the sun." Today we try to spend our way to happiness with more than the writer could have imagined, yet end up at the same place, a vague discontentment. Lexus cars had a commercial years ago that said people who say that money can't buy happiness were not spending it in the right place. I would agree with part of that assessment, although not with their proposed solution.

One thing I have noted, with dismay, is a societal shift that is exacerbating our financial problems. Past generations of Americans spent years saving for a down payment on a home. Cars, appliances, and electronics were bought only after a significant portion, if not all, of the purchase amount was saved for. An emergency fund was frequently built up and a nest egg established. Today's youth are now often demanding houses, cars, and electronics soon after graduation. Their nest egg is their fifth credit card, and their emergency fund is moving back in with their parents. Often it doesn't even occur to them that they have forfeited their next decade to their educational loans. It just seems to be the normal path of life to them.

The Business World and Christianity

Luke 16:14 mentions in passing that the Pharisees loved money. In the verse before that Jesus tells us we cannot serve both God and money. Essentially Jesus is telling us that money is an idol that those in His time, as well as today, and most certainly in the future, worship.

Financial gain is the driving factor of our modern economy and much of world history. Christian civilizations have thrived and spread the Gospels to all mankind, as directed in the Great Commission, in parallel with commerce and economic growth.

How can a Christian reconcile the warning from Jesus Himself and the necessity of serving Him with our stewardship of personal, family, national, and world finances?

Let's look for a moment at our God-bestowed economic and business systems. He Himself has granted us its immense riches and saw that we were born into a society with wealth beyond belief to any who trod the earth when His Son trod the earth. It was no mistake that He placed each of us into this era and its world economy.

Modern businesses often claim to work for the betterment of society and that they enrich all they touch. Many times, this is true. The services they provide are useful and needed by ordinary people. Lives are enhanced and families are supported by their services and goods.

A profit from their activities is required to continue their work and is often well deserved. They are to be congratulated for their efforts and success. Yet at times, the element of greed can cause even the finest examples of Christian businesses to harm those whom are the most weak and vulnerable. The idol of money usurps the need to serve those who can only place two very small copper coins in the temple treasury. Indeed, those who willingly gave those coins are now the victims.

That the rich prey upon the poor for even greater financial gain was old news when much of the Old Testament was written. No doubt it will also be the same until the Second Coming.

The most disheartening stories are when the poorest and the elderly in society are financially harmed simply to boost a business' bottom line a fraction of a percent. Could this be what Jesus meant by serving the idol of money instead of God?

A very depressing story was reported by the *Los Angeles Times* in their article on senior citizens being charged tens of thousands of dollars by hospitals and doctors who deliberately bypassed Medicare, which so many the elderly depend on. https://www.latimes.com/opinion/story/2019-12-20/medicare-coverage-hospitalization-patient-costs.

By having the elderly hospitalized as "outpatients" under "observation status," often for days, they bypass their "admission" and having the patient therefore eligible for Medicare payments. They can then charge that senior citizen more than Medicare allows and it then must be shouldered entirely by that elderly, ill person and their spouse. Many, if not most, senior citizens could be in the position of having one hospital "observation" financially ruin the rest of their and their spouse's lives. The article points out that some hospitals place up to seventy percent of their patients into the "observation status." I told my sister, who has spent her life in healthcare, primarily with the elderly, of my amazement. She was amazed that I was amazed, having seen, to her sorrow, financial ruin for her elderly patients for many years. Two-thirds of all bankruptcies are caused by health-care costs and my sister had seen it first-hand for decades. https://www.cnbc.com/2019/02/11/this-is-the-real-reason-most-americans-file-for-bankruptcy.html

Why would God allow thousands upon thousands of ill, elderly people to be ruined financially by these hospitals' practices? Why would God allow thousands to be conned out of their life savings through scam phone calls? Why would He let young families be scammed by salesmen selling investments that are worthless?

These issues are where the rubber meets the road when speaking of Christianity as a way of life. We may ignore or deny the impact of these, saying it impacts the other guy, not me. We may not want to take a stand, but look away because we don't want to be involved.

Did Jesus not want to be involved with the money changers who had made His Father's house a den of thieves? Did He know His outburst upon them would turn these wealthy men against Him and solidify their hatred upon what He was and said? They were wealthy and He was not. They were influential and He was a serious troublemaker. He was costing them money and, in their financial eyes, there could be no greater sin against them.

Clearly, satan is alive and doing well on planet Earth. Money may turn out to be his single most successful tool over the centuries and over souls. It is deeply concerning that personal and corporate wealth has become even more paramount today than it was in my youth.

It will be for the youth of today, who, in claiming Christianity as their way of life, to decide upon the paths, policies, and plans of their businesses, their society, and their lives. They will decide where Christian values, personal honor, compassion for those Jesus came to serve, and profit margin each belong. Two-thousand years ago a man told us we must either serve His Father or money. Each generation since then has had to make their decision on this never-ending question. The decisions of today's youth will be paid for by them at the price of courage.

Fairness

One of the first terms that comes up when discussing money and income is the word "fairness."

There isn't (much of) any.

A person can have a PhD in Divinity, blow the end off an IQ test, and work a legitimate sixty to seventy-hour work week for a decade and still be eligible for food stamps and the local food bank.

Their neighbor could have dropped out of high school, had a friend teach them how to drive a truck, and are able to afford a swimming pool that could hold all three of their new monster pickups.

My family knew a woman who ran a glue machine in a woman's shoe factory – until they won over a million dollars in a lottery.

A recent radio news story told of a single woman with children who had a good job and apparently was making a very fine income. At the end of the story we were told that she had fallen in love with a man in an online dating service and somehow managed to fraudulently obtain and send him over half a million dollars – in Nigeria.

As noted, there isn't (much of) any in terms of fairness.

The Lord causes some to work hard for their daily financial bread. He allows some to inherit billions. He arranges for some to be born into the British monarchy. He causes some to be born into a life of ill health in the ghetto.

His purposes are unfathomable to us, but He does have purposes and they are individual for each of us. We can attempt to learn His unique, loving path for us by reading and employing what is in this book, learning His Bible well, and trusting in Him. But fairness does not seem to be a factor.

It is easy to get wrapped up in the term "fairness." That word may turn out to be nothing more than the word "detour" in its heavenly translation. It can take us off His path and purpose for us with the anger, depression, despair, and hate it can generate.

We can howl and scream all we want about financial inequality, but what is the point? More to the point, does it matter? What matters is us individually as souls and how money affects us during our few short years under the sun. God will not welcome a corporation into heaven. The super-rich will be greeted in paradise alongside that school teacher who barely scrapped by on earth. The person who was born into a lifetime of luxury will kneel at our Lord's feet beside the widow who gave two very small copper coins to the temple treasury.

Do not be surprised if the widow is kneeling in a pew closer to the Lord.

Acceptance and a determination to serve Him and serve Him well may move us past this possible detour.

Guardianship of Finances

So, what are we to do about this Hydra called finances?

Many of us were given poor or no guidance on how to handle money while growing up. Our parental influences may have been limited to the boom and bust of spending and scrimping. Many of us were shielded from knowing anything about our family's finances and then expected to be wise stewards of money when we were on our own for the first time.

I remember vividly my father saying how wonderful credit cards were. You got all this great stuff and only had to pay the minimum amount each month. I also remember he worked two jobs for most of his years to keep our family afloat financially.

Often parents have no idea how to prepare their children for financial realities. One notable exception comes from one of the richest men in the world in their time. Governor and Vice President Nelson Rockefeller described how his father taught his children how to handle money. The John D. Rockefeller Jr's children were to keep an account of every penny of their simple allowance. They were given twenty-five cents with a bonus for work performed at their home. They were to donate ten percent of this amount to charity, save ten percent, and be able to account for how they spent the remainder (Maldonado). He wanted to instill in them a foundation of giving to charity and of saving money that he felt they would need throughout their lives.

Responsibility, prudence, and common sense may well be the foundations we need. Luke 16:11 tells us, "So if you have not been trustworthy in handling worldly wealth, who will trust you with true riches?" Obviously, worldly wealth is not true riches. God may define our personal riches in terms of raising Christian children, a life of health, a family we love, friends we enjoy, and a firm foundation of living a God-centered life. Money may well be a minor entry in our ledger.

Our Bible can serve as a guide. I remember reading of one unexpected use of the Bible to instill a lesson on finance. I read of a young lady, off to college for the first time, who was given a Bible by her father just as they left her dorm room. Sometime later, she told her parents she needed money, and her father sent her a list of ten Bible verses she should read in her new Bible. She later pleaded again for money and was given the same list of verses. On a phone call, she begged for money and was asked if she had read the verses. She swore she had, and her father said, "Oh no, you did not!" "I did," she insisted. The father retorted, "I know you didn't because I put twenty-dollar bills at each of the ten verses." The Bible may not hold dollar bills for us, but its guidance on money is invaluable.

Among the Biblical admonitions on finances, we are asked to provide our church with a tithe of what we make. The Lord himself doesn't need the cash, but He does need His people to have self-discipline and humility with what they do have.

Our greatest financial challenge is not with money, but how we behave with money. Are we serving God with what we have? Do we act responsibly toward our family and friends in our use of money? Are we trustworthy and honest in our financial dealings? Are our priorities Christian-based?

We may be generous to a fault with our bank accounts or stingy to the nth degree. Extremes are sharp edges that cut to the quick when we wander onto them. Ecclesiastes 7:18 tells us, "It is good to grasp the one and not let go of the other. Whoever fears God will avoid all extremes."

Being a good guardian with money is one of the hardest parts of being an adult, and it will define, to a certain extent, how good of an adult one turns out to be. Being content with what one has might be a new idea in one's life or one as ancient as the Bible. As noted earlier, Ecclesiastes 5:18-20 says, "This is what I have observed to be good: that it is appropriate for a person to eat, to drink, and to find satisfaction in their toilsome labor under the sun during the few days of life God has given them – for this is their lot. Moreover, when God gives someone wealth and possessions, and the ability to enjoy them, to accept their lot and be happy in their toil – this is a gift of God. They seldom reflect on the days of their life, because God keeps them occupied with gladness of heart."

Savings and Retirement

We are called upon, as guardians of our finances, to set aside money so as to not be a burden to our families when retirement is reached, or emergencies occur. In that same vein, various insurances seem to be required. I read over a decade ago that for an individual to live without health insurance, they would need access to three million dollars for catastrophic illnesses. Today, that figure could easily be double. Further, liability coverages can ward off the pitfalls that occur when lawyers are determined to sue you. Having insurance may be your only hope when you see what befalls some families.

Dave Ramsey, in his excellent ministry of financial peace, emphasizes having an emergency fund, as well as investments. Proverbs 13:11 indicates the savings path prudent for most of us, "Dishonest money dwindles away, but whoever gathers money little by little makes it grow." Investments in a 401k or IRA during our working years can be a wise and responsible choice for ourselves and our families. Arguably, the most significant benefit is not the money that is saved, but the discipline involved in saving.

You will no doubt run into many offers to make large amounts of money very quickly peddling snake oil. But who needs a well-oiled snake?

As noted earlier, "There is no free lunch, but for the rest of your life, someone will offer you one." But is that God's intended path for you and your family? Get rich quick schemes are usually just that - a scheme. You may wear your hands to the bone attempting to get rich in some cleaver scheme or find yourself duped by someone cleverer than you. Proverbs 23:4 counsels us, "Do not wear yourself out to get rich; do not trust in your own cleverness."

So, how should we invest our money? Ecclesiastes 11:2 advises us as today's financial planners do, to diversify our holdings so as to lessen our risk, "Invest in seven ventures, yes, in eight; you do not know what disaster may come upon the land."

We have been told all our lives that patience is a blessing. Billionaire Warren Buffett rephrased it best in his 1996 annual letter to shareholders, "If you aren't willing to own a stock for ten years, don't even think about owning it for ten minutes."

Help with Financial Problems

Any discussion of financial responsibility should begin with the financial ministry of Dave Ramsey. His lucid, down-to-earth approach to money has saved countless individuals, marriages, and families. A strong measure of financial sanity can be achieved from his Financial Peace University classes. Many churches provide these classes as a service to their congregations and communities.

For those who are seemingly addicted to debt, the Debtors Anonymous twelve-step program can provide a life-changing approach to the seemingly endless cycle of debt. Their web site can guide you to a local chapter.

We may find we were given no training on how to handle money and lack any reasonable guidance from family or friends. Frugality may need to rule our actions, as well as emotions, on this topic. Books and websites are available to help guide you on the financial course you are obliged to travel. Consider Dave Ramsey's books as your starting point.

Puzzle Pieces

Consider the following:

- What are three examples in your personal life that show the type of guardian you are of your money?
- What did your parents tell you about money when you were a child? Did they actually do what they told you to do?
- What examples did you have growing up on how to handle finances?
- Have you been able to save money? If so, where is it?
- Looking at your current debts (credit cards, cars, etc.), how many years will it take to pay them off by making minimum payments? (Credit card statements may provide this information.)
- How will you keep your credit card debt from rising?
- What expenses (medical, car, housing, appliances, etc.) will be coming in the next twelve months?
- How old will you be when you pay off your credit cards and other debts (car, house, etc.)?
- Have you ever become emotionally upset by what you or your spouse did with money?
- Did you ever have buyers regret when you made a purchase?
- How anxious are you about your financial situation?
- How will you use money to serve the Lord on your life path?

The point here is not only to have you review your financial health, but to see how money affects your personality, morals, life, and relationships.

10. Dreams, Sleep, and Health

Dreams

One easily overlooked facet of our lives, yet one that played a vital part in the Bible, is dreams. Frequently in the Bible, people were given directions for themselves, their families, and their nation through dreams. Today, we can also use dreams to help guide us to the path and destiny we are meant to fulfill. Further, we should not limit ourselves to the nighttime variety, but include the frequent wanderings of our minds while awake to understand ourselves better. Ralph Waldo Emerson said it best, "A man is what he thinks about all day long."

Wishful thinking, daydreams, and nighttime dreams can all be indicators of our current emotional state and projected path in life.

Sleep researchers tell us that our night dreams help our mind organize what happened during the previous day. Perhaps more importantly, they can also provide us with creative thinking, novel answers to problems, and personal guidance.

Supposedly we dream each night, but often we seem to have an avalanche of dreams when we are preoccupied with problems or concerns. Ecclesiastes 5:3 tellingly begins, "A dream comes when there are many cares."

Elias Howe, inventor of the sewing machine, was perplexed by the problem of attaching thread to a needle. One night he dreamed of cannibals who were preparing to cook him and were brandishing spears with holes on the ends. In the morning, he cooked up a solution to his problem by placing a hole at the end of a needle (List of dreams, 2016).

Prophetic dreams include New York lawyer Isaac Frauenthal who dreamt of the RMS *Titanic*, that he was to sail on, sinking. He was one of the few survivors (List of dreams, 2016).

Abraham Lincoln, on the day he was assassinated, told his bodyguard, William H. Crook, that he had been having dreams of being assassinated for three straight nights.

More recently, a Nobel laureate confessed that many years ago, he was debating whether to follow a career in English or science. He had a dream that he was a college professor of English and went to his class, and not a single student showed up. He took that to mean that he should follow a career in science, which led to his award.

The 1975 number one song, "Wildfire," by Michael Martin Murphey, came to him in its entirety in a dream. The melody to the song "Yesterday" was likewise born of a song. (List of dreams, 2016).

The Bible recounts how Joseph, Jesus' step-father, had a series of dreams that ensured the safety of baby Jesus. Joseph's first dream instructed him to take Mary as his wife. Later he was told to flee to Egypt, then to go to the land of Israel, and finally to not go to the land of Judea.

Genesis tells of the Old Testament Joseph whose life and the Bible were mightily changed because of a dream he had in his youth, then later his interpretations of dreams.

Similarly, we know from Matthew 2:12 that the Magi were told in a dream to return to their lands using a different route.

Matthew 27:19 narrates how Pilate's wife suffered a great deal that day because of the dream she had about that innocent man, Jesus.

I remember when I accepted Christ as my personal savior that the moment was similar to that described by C.S. Lewis when he realized Jesus was the Son of God. It was more like a man lying in bed asleep, then realizing he was awake. It was a calm, serene moment. Yet that night was the exact opposite. I dreamed of prophets from the Old Testament and apostles from the New Testament in a room on the second floor of an old country house. They were hysterically screaming and praising God. I was so unnerved by them that I went out a window onto a branch of a large, majestic tree. From inside they told me that was fine, I didn't have to be inside with them at that time. Later I interpreted the dream to mean that I was indeed saved, but that my coming inside to the world of the Bible and active Christianity would come later. Meanwhile, I would be on a branch of His tree of life. A piece of my life puzzle had been filled in.

As I was making my final edits to this book and preparing it for publication, a strange and concerning dream came to me that seemed instructive, so it is a last-minute addition.

I was in a strange city many hours from home on a business trip. I ran into an older businessman in a gray suit. He had been observing me apparently doing something. I had vaguely been aware of his watching, although it did not matter to me. He came up and very kindly, and clearly out of concern, told me that what I had been doing (whatever it was) could be seen as wrong, possibly insulting, or even offensive to another person. I politely, but firmly, told him no. I had no intention of wrongdoing, being rude, or affronting others. I thanked him and said I understood how others could misinterpret my actions or whatever, but I was a very strong Christian and he was simply misreading whatever I was doing. He then told me that how I am perceived by others is absolutely critical. How others see me and interpret what I am doing may be of far greater weight than any intention I may have. or even my message. What I do may not be wrong in mind, purpose, or action, but I must have some propriety in other people's eyes. I must unambiguously be seen as serving the Lord.

I was very puzzled by this. He then talked about the importance of how we appear to others and five or six other related things. I then realized that I was in the presence of an immense giant of Christianity and living it as a way of life. I wondered if they were an archangel or possibly Jesus Himself. I was stunned and amazed.

I thanked him profusely and told him I had to leave for a long trip back to my family. It was the afternoon and I wanted to return that night. He said that was fine, but there were other people I needed to talk to first. Again, I was very puzzled.

Suddenly, there was a middle-aged woman I had never met before next to me. There was also a young adult woman who was the daughter of a dear Christian couple I knew. I knew this young adult woman, who I will call H, when she was younger, but had not met her since she was a teenager. Like her parents, she was a good strong Christian and I thought very highly of her. She was with another woman her age that I was introduced to. The middle-aged woman and the younger ladies then took me to two or three Christian group meetings which I knew lasted several hours, but were over in the dream in a split second.

I was then deeply torn between driving back to my family, which included relatives both living and dead, that night or staying the night locally. It was starting to get dark. The three, especially the middle-aged woman, wanted me to stay. I told them I needed to get my many suitcases into my car. We walked toward it and I placed them in the trunk. I was still torn, but then I said that I would probably stay the night at a nearby hotel and see them for breakfast in the morning.

As we were talking in the parking lot, a massive, raging bull started to come toward us. I saw it first and yelled to the three, "Bull, bull, bull, let's get out of here! Let's get back! Everyone get inside!" We went inside a building through a glass door and watched it through a wall of glass. The ferocious bull had terrifying eyes. It seemed it could see completely through you and down into the deepest core of your soul. The bull was black, but the eyes were black beyond human belief. Humans could not understand how unthinkably black its eyes were. The bull's body was rampaging and damaging the cars in the lot, but somehow its head and eyes were frozen and locked looking directly into my eyes. The eyes showed a hatred that was so pure it was beyond anything humans could know.

In the parking lot, a friend of mine came out and said he would capture the evil beast. He had a special type of car he was using and went toward the bull to drive it away. The vicious bull stormed toward my friend and injured him. Not to the point of death, but he was wounded enough he had to leave for shelter.

I was then somehow given a flame thrower and was told the flames were what was important. Only flames would work on the creature now. Whoever gave it to me emphasized tremendously the word flames. I used the flamethrower on the enraged bull. It curled up into a large black ball and died. Minutes later the flames died away and a charred ball of this vanquished enemy was left in the parking lot.

I told the three women that I would stay at a nearby hotel that night and would return to my family late tomorrow. I wanted to see the three for breakfast in the morning. I found myself very sad that the gentleman who was a giant of Christian revelation would probably not be joining us, but I hoped he somehow would be there.

After awakening the next morning, I spoke on the phone with my friend who had been injured by the bull in my dream. He had been terminated from his job the day before because of a driving incident. I never told him of the dream.

I interpreted this as an admonition that how I am perceived by others is vitally important. It is central to serving Him as Christianity as my way of life. I must not lose propriety, respectability, and modesty in the eyes of my fellow man or it will reflect on Christianity. My motives may be pure, but other souls will see my actions and judge our faith by what I display.

Other salient elements seemed to be the need to work with other Christians and the necessity of postponing future plans (my trip home) so as to engage in Christian fellowship (the three women I was told I needed to meet). The large amount of baggage could have been seen as my earthly life's baggage – emotional, physical, history, financially, etc. – that needed to be put into a trunk as I do more important things. The parking lot could have indicated delays I should not have made in writing this book. The decision to stay the night and have breakfast the next day with my new Christian friends could herald a new morning of the next stage of my life. The raging bull (who I believe was satan) and his hatred of me and all progeny of Adam, was terrifying. However, I was taught that satan can be scorched and defeated given the weapons God will provide when we are attacked.

Daydreams

We are encouraged in the Bible to use our thoughts to dwell on things that are excellent and praiseworthy. We are to learn from them to fill our lives with their goodness. We are told this directly in Philippians 4:8, "Finally, brothers and sisters, whatever is true, whatever is noble, whatever is right, whatever is pure, whatever is lovely, whatever is admirable – if anything is excellent or praiseworthy – think about such things."

It can be healthy to let our minds wander. Often, we remember things or have new ideas by allowing our minds to stroll over facets of our lives. Mind wanderings can lead us to new branches on our path. Daydreams, wishful thinking, and random musings seem to be hardwired into our beings. The Lord apparently placed these within us to serve a purpose, and we should explore them.

As our minds wander at work, school, and in our free time, we need to note not just specific items that crop up, but patterns and emotions that are built up. Do our thoughts end up in stressful situations, pleasant encounters, or simply a puzzling state of affairs? Are we tapping our toes, flexing our muscles, or in a relaxed body state? Do we keep returning to the same patterns of thought or new and novel paths? Do we find we keep telling ourselves the same lies about situations we feel powerless about? All are potential clues and guideposts to the pathways God has decided we are to go down.

We are encouraged to think of what is excellent and praiseworthy, and we can start our mind's treks by doing so. Meanwhile, when caught daydreaming in class, we can plead we were doing homework for a book we are working on.

Premonitions

One topic I will touch on briefly, because I have no personal experience with such, is the topic of premonitions. It may well be that the Holy Spirit endows certain people with premonitions that come true. The purpose of these we will probably never know, but they can be quite unnerving when they happen.

For example, one woman I knew, who had such premonitions in the past, had a dream that her son-in-law was killed in a car accident. She was disturbed enough to contact her daughter in a distant state the next morning. By the end of the day, he had drowned in an accident.

Still another woman I knew, again who had premonitions, was convinced she would win a lottery for a trip to Hawaii. Before the drawing took place, she made arrangements for time off work for the trip that she indeed won.

Sleep

Sleep not only provides the daily rest our bodies require, but can be a barometer of our emotional state and indicator of health issues. How we arouse at daybreak may be telling. Some of us are morning people who readily awaken and look forward to the first light of day. Still, others are night people who detest the morning alarm clock as an audial version of an electric cattle prod. Sometimes we find that the issue is not so much with ourselves, but with the situation we awaken to. When you have to get up for everyone except yourself, it can make for a rough start of the day.

Approximately a third of our lives are spent, hopefully, in restful slumber. Those of us with sleep issues will find that these can significantly impact the remaining two-thirds of our lives.

For decades, my sleep apnea would lead to groggy mornings and less productive work. Coffee, to me, became like blood to a vampire. After a sleep study and diagnosis, I began using a CPAP machine, which turned into a true Godsend. For me, it is like getting an extra hour of restful sleep each night.

Being good guardians of our bodies very much includes taking care of our sleep. We, too often, attempt to get by without a full eight hours of rest, and the results spill over into the rest of our day. A bed you sleep well in, and getting a fulfilling night of sleep, may be among the best investments you can make in your life.

Physical Health

Being good overseers of our lives very much means taking care of our physical health. Our health will impact what we can do and how well we do it. Regular exercise, reasonable eating habits, and stern limits on vices all seem required to maintain our health.

1 Corinthians 6:19-20 tells us, "Do you not know that your bodies are temples of the Holy Spirit, who is in you, whom you have received from God? You are not your own; you were bought at a price. Therefore, honor God with your bodies." So, we are called upon to keep our bodies in reasonable shape. The fallout from poor health can affect our mood, capabilities, and outlook toward life and others. With such a draining impact, we cannot neglect our health, either preventatively by maintaining an active life or in response to illnesses.

It is interesting that many of us seem to go to one extreme or the other in terms of how we react to sickness, particularly men. The opposites of crawling under the covers at the first sneeze or complete denial of a severe illness seem to be magnetic poles we are attracted to.

I am at the southern pole when it comes to such. One of my glaring weaknesses, that I seem to share with many, is my refusal to admit when sickness has gotten the best of me. I could be on life support and would show up ready for a full eight-hour work shift. I remember one lengthy episode at college, fighting a fever, chills, sneezing, and a litany of symptoms. The next morning, I coughed up a phlegm ball that would have done a rummy with a month old cold proud and went in for another full day at school. I probably infected most of the campus over the next few days, but I was not going to miss my classes. I survived, but would not wager on the prospects of my peers.

Although not a member, I have always held in high esteem those in the Jesus Christ Church of Latter-Day Saints for, among other things, how they maintain their bodies as temples to God.

I will admit that my aging temple to the Lord is presently in need of some restoration. As Orson Wells aptly put it, "Gluttony is not a secret vice." Losing a few pounds of temple expansion is not an easy task for some of us. I see exercise as a foul and onerous task that is part of the "howdy" level of Dante's *Inferno*. I partake of it on a semi-regular basis, with emphasis on the word "semi." Reluctantly, I get on my exercise machine and get off it smelling like a hot day at the zoo, but realize I am better off for it.

My father was a robust example of how not to live a healthy life and could not have cared less. When first diagnosed as a diabetic, the doctor asked him the usual questions about his lifestyle. When asked what he had for a typical breakfast, my father replied six Twinkies and two Pepsis. The doctor thought he was joking. Oh no, he was not.

Maintaining a healthy body, mind, and, by extension, soul, seems to be a requirement of our path in life. He made us to enjoy the benefits of a healthy body and, by exercising, we can feel the pleasure meant for us on that path. As Romans 12:1 says, "Therefore, I urge you, brothers and sisters, in view of God's mercy, to offer your bodies as a living sacrifice, holy and pleasing to God – this is your true and proper worship."

Mental and Emotional Health

Our mind is where we reside throughout our lives. Nothing else is as important when we attempt to find and serve the Lord. Our outlooks and moods will change as each day progresses. Our thoughts and emotions will largely dictate our actions as we muddle through our days. It is our mind where we actually reside. As quoted earlier, "A man is what he thinks about all day long."

We grapple with the emotions racing through our minds. We juggle many disjointed thoughts. We are depressed, and we are elated. We are anxious, and we know serenity. Everything we are is here. It is also where we worship our Lord, it is where satan attacks us, and it is where the Holy Spirit inspires us.

We swim in an ocean of emotions. Try going for one hour without some feeling or emotion. It is all but impossible and seems only to occur when we are truly engrossed in some activity. Even then, emotions readily slip in. Yet undeniably, as emotions slide in, we are given the freedom to choose our attitudes and outlooks. Emotions can be addressed with thoughts and actions based upon them decided. As noted in Philippians 4:11-13, Paul tells us, "I am not saying this because I am in need, for I have learned to be content whatever the circumstances. I know what it is to be in need, and I know what it is to have plenty. I have learned the secret of being content in any and every situation, whether well fed or hungry, whether living in plenty or in want. I can do all this through Him who gives me strength."

Paul had determined how his emotions should play out regardless of his circumstances. He took his freedom to choose his reactions to his situations and used it as a testimony to Christianity as a way of life.

If we are to keep healthy anywhere, it must be our minds. Clear thinking is required as we attempt to find our path. Emotions are to be recognized and can be used for guidance on our daily trek. Our intellect needs to be engaged as we chart our way forward. The interplay of thoughts and emotions is ground zero for what we are and what we are to become.

Our current and future actions may well be spawned from our emotional reactions to the stresses of life. Much of human history and our personal history has been generated by emotions and the actions they spurred. As with Paul, we must wisely choose how our emotions are acted upon so as to serve as a witness to our beliefs.

We will find that depression and anxiety will swell up at times. At others, we can have unreasonable euphoria. At still others, we obsess on things, both great and small. These may be due to our mental constitution, owing to external turmoil we find ourselves in, or because of the bad cucumber we had for lunch. Regardless, emotional upheavals will occur, and they will impact our thoughts and, through them, our reactions to the world.

Know that satan knows of your feelings and will use your mind as his battleground. Your thoughts are known to him and he will counter them with his own. Often these attacks are mere slivers of vices such as pride, greed, lust, and envy. They seem reasonable enough feelings at the time, but make you susceptible to more significant vices later. That wisp of envy as you hear of another's promotion can be exploited later. Our disdain for a welfare family at our church can be a stumbling block. Often satan sees time and setting up patterns of feelings and thoughts as his long-term advantage over us.

Sanity has been defined as reasonable behaviors, thoughts, and emotions. By maintaining reasonable ways, we help insulate ourselves from satan's attacks. When we tread to extremes, we have to be concerned about where we are going and who is doing the prodding. As noted, the Bible tells us to keep clear of extremes in Ecclesiastes 7:18, "It is good to grasp the one and not let go of the other. Whoever fears God will avoid all extremes." We must know how and when to react by attempting to choose our emotional responses and thoughts to life's many stresses.

A popular quote, with a number of variations, is "Hate is like drinking poison and hoping the other guy dies."

Extremism is a favored tool by satan, and he knows it is highly effective with social groups in general and your emotional health in particular. Ready-made to scrape against raw emotions, political and social groups sprouting extremism are easily found on today's internet, with people going to "news" sites for radicalization. As a measuring stick, the greater the intolerance for another group and the more vitriol, hate, and scorn spewed toward other people, the greater satan's success with that site and its adherents. The more we find ourselves in such company, the more we risk the loss of emotional health.

We may hate a political or social idea, but do we have to emotionally hate the people themselves for advancing such? That will depend on the true leader we follow– Jesus or satan.

A popular definition of insanity is doing the same thing over and over, yet expecting different results. It is also the way of the world. We spend too much money and wonder why we are fearful of checking our VISA accounts. We eat too much ice cream and can't understand why we can't lose weight. We once again have that fourth beer and are upset when our spouse once again asks for our car keys. We seem oblivious to the cycles we live. We can't understand why the law of cause and effect can't make an exception just this once. Why is that law so unreasonable to us personally? Maybe it was passed by Congress.

We must keep ourselves within reasonable thoughts, emotions, and actions. Adherents to the Alcoholics Anonymous and similar twelve-step groups often refer to their addictions as obsessions of the mind. All reasonableness is gone in their addicted minds. One such group, Emotions Anonymous, is even based on the unreasonableness of their emotions and their behaviors caused by those emotions. With advances in medicine, many of the innate biochemical propensities toward depression, anxiety, and euphoric episodes can be treated and made more reasonable. The obsessions can be made more rational. But the desire and decision for reasonableness will be ours to make.

1 Peter 1:13 comments on how our minds should be, "Therefore, with minds that are alert and fully sober, set your hope on the grace to be brought to you when Jesus Christ is revealed at His coming."

We are told that people who have a healthy support system with family and friends are emotionally more stable and healthier than those without such. This is echoed in the Bible as friendships are shown, strong family ties revealed, and groups, such as the apostles, presented. When his world crashed down around him, Job had the blessing of having three friends come and stay with him for seven days and nights.

As part of emotional and mental health, exercising our minds seems obligatory. Becoming a Christian will require you to keep as sharp a mind as you are able. How this is performed appears to be individually determined, although meditating on God's word through reading the

137

Bible is clearly required. Development of a quick and insightful mind is a blessing that we can all obtain to varying degrees. Reading and interactions with others can sharpen our minds and provide grist for the mental mill. The options are many, and your path will provide them as you start to own it. It will be up to you to decide what is best for your mind's health – video games or reading Christian books, TV reruns or a challenging online course, Hollywood gossip websites or learning more about your spouse's hobbies. You will be provided many options, and stewardship of your life and future will rest solely in your hands.

Near Death Experiences

One topic that has come up in the past several decades is that of near-death experiences (NDE). Some believe these are when people have reached a different state of being and had a direct connection with angels or even God. Others, though, deny that such a phenomenon exists.

I knew a devout Christian who had such an experience, and I feel I can trust in their word, although I will admit it could have been the result of a pain-killing drug-induced hallucination. They were driving in a snowstorm and were hit back to back by two drunk drivers. Badly mangled, my friend was taken to a hospital and had their NDE that night. They felt they floated toward a light and were met by a being who asked if they wished to go on or return to their life. In that she had two small children, she replied she wished to return. When asked why she said she had responsibilities. She immediately returned to her hospital bed. I know she was on strong pain-killers, but I also know my friend was a very honest Christian.

If these are experiences where we draw close to God, they are probably meant to instruct us. My friend felt the weight of responsibility for her children. Others feel similar needs when they "return." Some have claimed to have descended into hell and were rescued by Jesus. Regardless, these are possibly instructive to all. They help us realize that we must understand what is important to Him and live lives accordingly.

Puzzle Pieces

Consider the following:

- Do you have recurring dreams or dreams that follow some pattern? What would they be, and why do you think you have them?
- Have you ever had a dream that seemed intended to guide you in your life? Did you let it guide you or do you wish you had let it guide you?
- What emotions come to the fore when you dream?
- Do you usually have good, relaxing sleep each night?
- How do your daydreams end up? Are you stressed, relaxed, or a mixture of several emotions?
- Do your daydreams keep returning to the same situations or patterns of thought? If so, what are they?
- How do you feel after you exercise your body? Glad, irritated, pleased, or what?
- Do you find yourself gravitating toward what many call extreme social groups? Do they encourage anger, rage, and vitriol toward other people? How does that please satan?
- What do you do to maintain a healthy mind? Do you exhibit reasonable thoughts and behaviors?
- Is your emotional state usually stable? How do you handle situations that can cause emotional upheavals?
- How do other's negative words and actions affect your emotional state?

11. Virtues and Vices

To get a true puzzle picture of our path in life, we must view both the good and bad elements that comprise the person we are and are to be. We will now delve deeper into what constitutes our character. We must strip back and uncover those aspects of ourselves that might be just below our recognition. We will look at the good inherent within us and the bad that comprises part of our souls.

The ancients came up with the concept of the seven deadly sins, or vices, and the seven heavenly virtues. They are primary in that all forms of sin and virtues stem from these foundations. They are within us, and we can learn deeply about ourselves through studying them and how they have played out in our lives.

Although these lists have fluctuated some over the centuries, they are generally recognized today as the following:

Seven Deadly Sins: Pride, Envy, Gluttony, Greed, Lust, Wrath, and Sloth

Seven Heavenly Virtues: Chastity, Temperance, Charity, Diligence, Patience, Kindness, and Humility

With very few exceptions, we have all experienced these vices and virtues. They are faced daily and can take up a great deal of time and emotional effort. We will face them until the day we die.

Exercising each virtue and exercising each sin is not spiritual addition or subtraction, but multiplication or division. They are compounding events where performing a small series of virtues causes a multiplying of each in their impact on our souls and those we interact with. A series of sins divides and then divides again and continues to divide the strength of our souls against satan as more sins are acted upon. Repetition multiplies spiritual strength or causes moral decay. No weightlifter performs one bench press and expects muscles to appear. The cumulative effect of acting on virtues or sins builds what we will present to our God when we take our last breath.

Seven Deadly Sins

Sin is an abstract object to humans because we cannot see, hear, or touch it directly. We see actions and hear words that place sins on our souls, but not sin per se. We understand it stains our souls, that one and only portal we have to God for eternity. We know it caused dull nails to go through the hands and feet of a man two-thousand years ago. But we don't actually see it as God or satan clearly see it attached to our souls. Nor do we see their forgiveness that our Savor gained for us with the words, "Father, into your hands I commit my spirit."

Maybe the closest to a physical manifestation of sin that humans can understand are parasitic worms. Parasites not only crawl under your skin and eat your inner flesh, they also lay eggs inside you to hatch later as other sins and empty their feces that carry virus-borne diseases into your body tissue. Parasites most frequently eat away the brain, eyes, intestines, lungs, and skin. Their cure is by digging them out or heavy-duty medications. Reinfection of parasites and sin are common to the point of being expected. Basic hygiene and cleanliness are required to prevent continued, and more severe, infestations and rotted flesh from parasites. Living a clean Christian life is the basic hygiene needed to prevent further infestation of satan's parasites.

The seven deadly sins are evils that can come to us brutally hard, but more often are subtle and often masquerade as things we think we deserve. We see them as matters of pride or are feelings that are understandable given our situation. These prods to sin are frequently based on the cardinal sin of pride, but they can also come to us in the form of the lesser vices of envy, greed, and gluttony. The devil is not a fool; he knows that small sins can lead to greater ones and provides us with ample opportunities.

We may start with the sin of gluttony, then have our pride say that we are above that fault and that only lesser men than ourselves suffer from such afflictions. Gluttony is gone from the equation, but pride is now entrenched. We find that satan is perfectly happy to have the greater sin of pride used to push away the smaller sin of gluttony as brain cancer may replace a headache.

Pride

Pride is the first of the deadly sins, and it is first for a reason. Many of the other sins, to varying extents, can be traced back to this foundational sin. We know that satan became satan because of pride. It is a comparison sin in that with pride, we compare ourselves to others and then see these others as inferior. In worst cases, we act upon our imagined superiority. The greatest example of pride gone riot could be the Nazi movement of the last century. The supposedly master race was bent on annihilating the inferior Jewish race.

One of the easiest lies for a person to swallow is that they are somehow superior to another person, instead of being equal to them in the eyes of God. We may have better grades, a more athletic body, a keener mind, more money, a better job, as well as be more religious than a particular coworker, family member, neighbor, or person in another state. Still, it is all for naught when we are viewed by a dying man on a cross. To Him, we are seen as just another struggling, failing person whose soul He died to save. We have a soul He died for. Those whom we consider inferior also have a soul He died for. Jesus did not feel extra pain as the nails were driven in for us and less pain for them.

Social and internet groups spewing scorn, hatred, and vitriol at others of different races, religions, or political thought can serve satan and serve him well. Extremism and pride are combined by satan and inseparable with each other, as well as inseparable to satan's cravings for your soul.

The internet holds a horrific number of sites prodding hatred for God's beloved children. The race, creeds, ideology, and a thousand other illusions of how other human beings, made in God's image, are different than ourselves are presented and victimized. Jesus, who died for all mankind, and who in His very last words gave us His Great Commission for all races, must be in horror. Undoubtedly, satan must be deeply, deeply satisfied with what he has accomplished on these internet sites.

Vanity can be traced to pride, as can contempt, arrogance, conceit, lying, and a host of other spiritual ailments. Proverbs 16:5 is telling, "The

Lord detests all the proud of heart. Be sure of this: They will not go unpunished."

The remaining six of the seven deadly sins stem from our stem – our brain stem — the reptilian portion of our brain. We, like reptiles, have a brain stem that is responsible for our basic bodily needs. The six vices left are, to varying extents, corruptions of our physical needs. These corruptions are exaggerations of things leading to bodily and mental comforts. For example, envy can be for another person's prestige, money, looks, and sexual escapades. Greed maintains we should have all the clothing, jewelry, and alcohol our bodies can use and then much more. Gluttony ends with a full stomach, a rotund waistline, clogged arteries, and then it starts up again.

The devil is happy to see us use our brain stems to sink to reptilian status in our thoughts and actions. Know that he never forgot that we, not he the snake, were made in God's image.

Envy

Envy is the desire for the talents, qualities, status, goods, and situations we see in others. Again, it is a comparison sin, but this time we are the lesser ones. We feel inferior, and it stings. We often feel it is unfair that we got the dirty end of the stick in looks, abilities, and traits. The Holy Spirit granted us gifts, and we were given less than what we should have gotten, or even what we need.

The comparison is made worse in that we often compare our insides to others' outsides. The devil will prod us into that judgment where he knows we will lose. We feel stressed and inadequate in so many ways on our inside, and they, on their outside, have that job, looks, spouse, and money we so desire. Yet on the inside, they too are a stressed, inadequate person burdened with envy of those whom they compare themselves to. It never ends. One person will always find someone else to envy and to no avail other than bitterness, rage, and depression.

Proverbs 14:30 (ESV) states, "A tranquil heart gives life to the flesh, but envy makes the bones rot."

Gluttony

Gluttony is the desire to consume more than one requires. We can have voracious appetites for food and drink and, when looking in a mirror, understand the Orson Wells quote from earlier, "Gluttony is not a secret vice." But gluttony can take on many forms. We can see conspicuous consumption of money and goods for no purpose other than to up our pride as gluttonous. Excessive alcohol stands as a form of gluttony. The Alcoholics Anonymous program aptly tells us that one drink is too many and a million are not enough. Regardless of what we have, we will try to consume more.

Proverbs 28:7 informs us, "A discerning son heeds instruction, but a companion of gluttons disgraces his father."

Greed

Greed is the desire for material wealth, and we see it front and center on page one of the tabloids and thousands of web sites. Too much is not enough. The multi-millions of dollars are simply not adequate for some. They cannot buy as many Porsche's as are needed, clothing cannot be bought fast enough, and we absolutely must have the electronic toy of the week. Ironically this can lead to a mindset where the goods or money become secondary. The mega-fraudster Bernie Madoff apparently was caught up in the game of swindling money more than he was with the money. The money became less important, and the greed-based thrill became greater as time went on.

Greed and buying too much can also be just the beginning of a life butchering cycle. The buying high you get all too often leads to the financial plunge of being in debt. The best car, electronics, or vacation that a down payment can buy soon leads to a life of scraping to make minimum payments on our numerous credit cards.

I remember working in a financial institution where one wag changed computer DOS prompts to "Greed is good." More accurately, it should have been, "Greed can be a tool of satan."

Luke 12:15 states, "Then He said to them, 'Watch out! Be on your guard against all kinds of greed; life does not consist in an abundance of possessions.'"

145

Dan Boozan

Lust

Lust is an inordinate craving for sexual pleasures. The media knows well that sex sells and that programs featuring sexual misconduct often sell very well. The influence of these programs and associated print and internet media cannot be underestimated. Further, a societal shift seems to have occurred coming from pharmacology.

With the advent of oral contraceptives, a dragon of lust was released as sex became simply an exciting and adventuresome way of life. But where did this sexual experimentation lead?

Today we have a society that is comfortable with sex but has difficulty with love. The lessons of Sodom and Gomorrah were lost on a society that allows same-sex marriages. The horror of two-year-old boys being killed by Herod's troops some two thousand years ago has been replaced by the horror of forty-five million abortions. The concept of chastity has given way to AIDS for the millions.

2 Timothy 2:22 tells us, "Now flee from youthful lusts and pursue righteousness, faith, love, and peace, with those who call on the Lord from a pure heart."

Wrath

Wrath is anger inflicted on others. God showed his anger on His people when they bowed before strange gods. His Son raged against the money changers who made His father's house a den of thieves. Wrath has its time and place, but it is for specific times and places.

Today we are told we have the "right" to be angry for any minor slight. When a fellow college student insults our race, we demand the University president resign. If we are "dissed" by others, we have the right to pull a gun. When we use a device that all research shows is helpful, but is later found defective, we are pressed to enter a lawsuit to get a large cash settlement.

Wrath is now a commodity that is based on whims, fear, greed, and pride. Tit for tat we respond and escalate any minor inconvenience out of proportion.

Psalms 37:8 says, "Refrain from anger and turn from wrath; do not fret – it leads only to evil."

Sloth

Sloth is the avoidance of physical or mental work. We live in a bi-polar society that wants us to work sixty-hour weeks, but we see other workers telecommute so they can sleep in. We rush our children to their numerous activities but are frustrated when they play computer games instead of doing school work. We return from our jobs to several hours of household work while our spouse watches TV. Our jobs do not let us get enough sleep, and we criticize that lazy welfare family who sleeps in instead of going to church. Sloth is hard for us to come by personally, but we see it continuously in others.

We often see others as slothful, but then either exempt ourselves from such judgment or castigate ourselves as being such. We may define our days off as time and rest well deserved, or we may feel guilty that we aren't accomplishing more. Often, we do both. What we need is a balance. We need to understand that we were given the seventh day as one of rest. Often our priorities need to be established with respites on our daily path, but diligence on our lifelong path.

Proverbs 15:19 says, "The way of the sluggard is blocked with thorns, but the path of the upright is a highway."

Seven Heavenly Virtues

Whereas the seven deadly sins have been hardbound for centuries, their opposition, the virtues, have had many incarnations. Some strictly list Faith, Hope, and Charity. Others give the four cardinal virtues of prudence, temperance, courage, and justice. Still, others counterbalance the seven deadly sins with Chastity, Abstinence, Liberality, Diligence, Patience, Kindness, and Humility. However, a grouping of seven virtues, known commonly as the seven heavenly virtues, will be used here. They consist of Charity, Temperance, Chastity, Diligence, Patience, Kindness, and Humility.

Charity

Charity, we are told in 1 Corinthians 13:13 (KJV), is the greatest of faith, hope, and charity. We can find the essence of charity in the Greek term "agape," an unselfish love for our fellow man. We see this demonstrated by generosity and altruistic giving. Jesus, in Luke 21:1-4, spoke of the poor widow who gave two copper coins to her temple and noted she gave out of her poverty, unlike those who gave much and much lorded it over others. During the week that I am writing this, a news article was published by a respected business journal. It listed the twenty wealthiest people in America, their worth, and the amount of that that they gave to charity the previous year. Only three gave over one percent. The average of the remaining seventeen was 0.3 percent. The richest person in the world only gave 0.1 percent to charity. The average American gives 3.7 percent to charities, including churches.

In the traditional sense, charity speaks of an unlimited, loving kindness toward all others regardless of circumstances. We see this exemplified in the lives of individuals such as Mother Teresa, who saw the Lord's face in those she ministered to. An element of humility is contained within charity, and it can be practiced by giving others our time and assistance. We can stand up for the rights of others when we exercise charity.

This is among the easiest, yet commonly bypassed, actions that can be undertaken in living Christianity as a way of life. Complementing the janitor at work, assisting someone in reaching for an item on the top shelf at the grocery store, bringing snacks to the office during a particular busy time, and a thousand more opportunities are provided by God for you.

Christmastime brings a great need for charity and provides opportunities to serve God through providing for others. For twenty-five years I have given gifts to children who would not have a single gift for Christmas through angel trees, usually through the Salvation Army. Children in destitute homes provide volunteers with a list of one or more items they would like to have on the day our Savior was born. These items are written on paper ornaments and become available in malls, churches, and other places. People then serve the Lord by buying these gifts for the children and giving them to the volunteers who then see that the children have the gifts. Children and adults alike can then better see the association between the ultimate gift God the Father gave us with His Son and the gifts we give on the celebration of this supreme moment of God's love.

Toys for Tots is wonderfully similar program and is run by the U.S. Marine Corps. In my state of Georgia, the state Division of Family and

Children Services has a similar program for foster children called the Secret Santa program. Other states may have similar programs. Churches and charities may also have such opportunities for you to serve the Lord.

A family with a special needs child or special needs adult often need assistance all year round and a small birthday gift or gift for no reason may be a small purchase for you, but can have an immense impact on them.

The Lord often calls on us and we must decide if we are to answer. For all eternity, He will never forget that ten-second moment you stooped to help one of His children. We must think long and hard of how we want Jesus to remember us for all eternity. After we pass this mortal life, He will know us for all time as the person who provided a gift to a small, scared, and lonely child one Christmas.

Temperance

Temperance contains elements of self-restraint, abstention, and moderation. Here we have the judgment for appropriate actions at appropriate times. There is a proper balance between self-interest and the needs of others. All things that are permitted are undertaken in moderation.

Often associated with abstention from alcohol, its influence can also be felt as we reign in greed and gluttony from their excesses. Temperance in emotions should also be considered as anger, and emotional outbursts are prevented. Rechanneling extravagances and extremes to moderation are practiced using temperance.

Fairness in our dealings with others is seen here, as is reasonableness and equality. We will stand up for ourselves when we judge it necessary but consider other's needs at the same time.

Chastity

Chastity is seen as abstaining from sexual conduct outside of marriage. I have said that young couples, when becoming more serious with each other, should often and very frankly talk about sex. Although in some cases over trans-Atlantic phone calls.

However, chastity also reaches much deeper. A moral wholesomeness is obtained with chastity that touches on honesty with others, integrity in business dealings, and honor in our family life. Here we maintain a moral high ground to withstand society's immoral callings. We can see chastity in the refraining from intoxicants, temptations, or corruptions on our path.

Diligence

Diligence is a zealous, conscientious nature to one's actions and work. There is a decisive work ethic, reliability, and resoluteness in beliefs. Here we see the wisdom of budgeting time and guarding against sloth. A component of integrity is ingrained in this virtue. Honesty, truth, and honor can be seen as elements of diligence.

Patience

Patience leads us to acceptance, forbearance, and strength in dealing with others. We resolve issues and conflicts peacefully. Forgiveness, mercy, and stability are facets of patience. We know serenity, perseverance, and fortitude when we practice patience. We find toleration of others, their lives, and their beliefs here.

Kindness

Kindness contains elements of charity, as well as compassion and friendship. Empathy and trust are practiced without resentment. Unselfish love and a cheerful demeanor are seen in moments of kindness. We can serve as an inspiration to others when we practice kindness. Sympathy, when appropriate, and thoughtfulness can be provided to our fellow man through kindness.

Humility

Humility is modest behavior, unselfishness, and having respect for others. It is not thinking less of yourself, but of thinking of yourself less. Humility contains the attitude needed to be a learner and shows reverence for wisdom. It contains the dedication and strength needed to undertake arduous, thankless tasks. Humility requires we renounce pride and be faithful to obligations. We are able to confront fear and uncertainty with a humble attitude.

Humility is the antithesis of pride and serves as its antidote. 1 Peter 5:5 tells us, "In the same way, you who are younger, submit yourselves to your elders. All of you, clothe yourselves with humility toward one another, because, 'God opposes the proud but shows favor to the humble.'"

Courage

I will end the discussion on these virtues by pointing out a special virtue that has a unique position. The tangent point between each virtue and its opposing sin is the element, emotion, or occurrence of courage. Standing on the crevasse's edge, even a modicum of courage can shift our balance so as to remain true to a specific virtue and prevent a fall into the juxtaposition sin. The least tincture of bravery can immunize us from a deadly sin that satan has worked weeks in your mind on.

C.S. Lewis summarizes this common miracle called courage, "Courage is not simply one of the virtues, but the form of every virtue at the testing point." He also noted that Pilate had the courage to stand up to the Pharisees – until it became risky.

Puzzle Pieces

In assessing our internal constitution, we need to perform an honest, searching, and fearless moral inventory of ourselves. This is as important as our listing of innate personality traits in knowing the framework of our lives and our future. Our Life Puzzle will not be complete until we have done so.

Consider the following:

- Which of the deadly sins are most apparent in your life today and in your past?
- How have they manifested themselves in your life? Pride, lying, cheating, stealing, arrogance, belittling others?

- Thinking of the coming week, which ones will satan probably bring before you? Can you plan ahead how you will react?
- Which of the heavenly virtues are most apparent in your life today and in your past?
- What are some examples of how you exercised these virtues? Giving time to others, undertaking difficult tasks for the benefit of others, standing up for others, compassion, showing mercy?
- Thinking of the coming week, can you plan on using one for a specific situation you will face?

12. Prayer

Prayer is our means to express to the Lord our praise, thoughts, hopes, and fears. Some are brief, while others span pages. The purpose and meaning can be very specific, or we can simply offer them to God with no agenda in our hearts.

We have special prayers for meals, church services, weddings, baptisms, etc. Mark 9:29 tells us that demons can be driven out by prayer.

When we pray, the Holy Spirit intervenes on our behalf to God. Romans 8:26 – 27 tells us, "In the same way, the Spirit helps us in our weakness. We do not know what we ought to pray for, but the Spirit himself intercedes for us through wordless groans. And he who searches our hearts knows the mind of the Spirit, because the Spirit intercedes for God's people in accordance with the will of God."

This tells us we do not have to know what to pray for, but that the Holy Spirit will intercede for us in accordance with the will of God for us. Our prayers are heard.

The Bible also tells us we can forcefully go to God in prayer for specific reasons. Philippians 4:6-7 states, "Do not be anxious about anything, but in every situation, by prayer and petition, with thanksgiving, present your requests to God. And the peace of God, which transcends all understanding, will guard your hearts and your minds in Christ Jesus." So, we know we can boldly go through prayer to God's throne of grace and request mercy in our times of need.

We often present our requests before God for things, both great and small. Sometimes they seem answered, sometimes obviously not. Regardless, they are heard.

One can have the illogical thought that they can pray enough to reach the amount God requires to perform some action for them. God wishes to give many blessing to us, but only in accordance with His purposes for us and our fellow man.

153

One thing that most of us never consider is that we can find ourselves drawn to specific prayers. Twelve-step members adhere to what is commonly called the Serenity Prayer. Fishermen for centuries have prayed, "Dear Lord, be good to me. The Sea is so wide and my boat is so small." Still others have found comfort in the Psalms snippet, "Be still and know that I am God." The apostles were instructed to pray what is known as the Lord's Prayer. Still, there are many other prayers we find in Christendom, including those we improvise as situations darken around us.

What are these prayers we say, and why are we drawn to specific ones? Are there Biblical passages and prayers with particular meanings that beckon us on our path? What clues can we find from them?

If you find yourself attracted to a specific prayer, it may well be that the Holy Spirit is calling you toward it for your own benefit and for purposes you may never fully understand. Here, we will consider a few prayers and a variation of a popular prayer. We will see how God may be calling upon you through them as you use them in calling upon God.

You will need to answer for yourself which prayers you find yourself resorting to when anxious, in need, or are emotionally drained. The ones that offer comfort at those times can also provide puzzle pieces about your life.

What we may not realize is that possibly prayer's greatest impact is not that it changes God, but that it changes us. We learn humility, patience, and a measure of serenity through prayer. In prayer we are acknowledging Him as our all-powerful creator and admit how minor we are. Regardless of any overt response from Him, He loves us, He hears us, and He will help us on our path toward Him.

What is key is not so much the words, but our heart's position at the time we utter a prayer. The words simply help focus that heartbeat. If the words were the only thing that mattered, an endless loop of prayers generated on your laptop would place it in heaven far ahead of any human soul.

The Lord's Prayer

Most readers probably pray daily, and most of those who do probably pray what is called the Lord's Prayer. This prayer was taught by Jesus to

His disciples and is also called the Disciples Prayer. It is used universally throughout Christian denominations.

When Jesus told his followers these precious words, it was one of the defining moments in Christ's ministry. It was a revelation and a revolution. This was one of the new rules of a new world. More would come, but this was a foundation they had to know and understand to follow Him. I doubt that another day went by that the disciples did not say it or puzzle over its meanings.

Some would call this a fragmented prayer. I say fragmented because it deliberately jumps between many topics, like a precious diamond having many facets that reflect and enhance each other's beauty.

This diamond is a model of brevity and power. Its sixty-eight words can be broken into multiple facets that shed light on its many purposes. It instructs us, has us implore Him, and grants us knowledge of His nature. It is worth noting that Jesus, His one and only son, taught us to pray it in the plural.

There are variations recorded in Matthew and Luke, but here we will use a common version used by many denominations.

Our Father,

The first two words Jesus taught us tell us that we are to refer to Almighty God, the maker of all creation, and He who destroyed all mankind, save Noah and his family, as our father. This could be seen as the height of insolence, yet we are commanded to do so. He wants us to know Him as our personal father, and He will treat us as His beloved children. His love is a father's love, not a mother's love for us. He would rather not, but will not spare the rod in any necessary discipline.

Who art in heaven,

Next, we are told where our Father exists. He created heaven as a final resting place for us to be with Him for time without end. He feels it is vital for us to understand that there is a heaven, and He exists not only with us today, but will with us in heaven for eternity.

Hallowed be thy name

This is followed by a command to honor His name. Given that we cannot directly see or touch God, our means of identifying Him is through the use of His name. We are to revere it in all its forms. As God or Lord or Yahweh, we are to acknowledge the power and majesty of Him through how we use His name. He knows instantly when we use His name and how it was used.

Thy kingdom come,

How is the Lord's kingdom to come into our world? Through the second coming of Jesus Christ seems obvious. Not only is this an affirmation, but one stated by God's son. At my age, as of this writing, I don't think I will live to see this occur, but I may not miss it by much.

So how does this instruct us in this current era? Perhaps we are to act as if His kingdom had come. John 13:35 tells us what we should know, "By this everyone will know that you are my disciples, if you love one another."

We are to hold Christianity as a way of life, and our interactions with others are to be a testimony to that. We are His beloved children, and we are to sit up straight and act as such.

Thy will be done, on earth as it is in heaven.

Here we are asked to do our Lord's will on earth as it is performed in heaven. So how is His will done in heaven? I will assume angels perform His will both instantly and perfectly. So how is His will done on earth by us? Hesitatingly and flawed come to mind.

But He made us as the hesitating and flawed human race and loves it when we try to make an effort, much as a father is proud of their child trying to make their first hesitating and flawed first steps. He knows us and will work through us, granting us direction and the means to do His will on earth. With His help, we make our hesitating and flawed steps to love one another.

Often His daily will for us, personally, is as simple as complementing the office janitor, cleaning the office break room, or not arguing with our children. Often, we fail, but sometimes we succeed. Regardless, He loves us.

Give us this day, our daily bread

Here we implore God to grant us what we need for this particular day. The ancients ate bread as their daily sustenance across all classes and cultures. So, in this appeal, we ask for what we need to carry out His will today. We ask for that spiritual food that will nourish our souls, grant us the ability to do His will, and give us the strength to accomplish His plan for us. We ask for what we need, not necessarily what we want. God is not the great go-fer to bring us the riches we desire, but His steadfast love for us will provide us with a string of mercies, grace, and the bread we need this very day.

And forgive us our trespasses as we forgive those who trespass against us

Our offenses and sins against God and those whom He loves are now faced directly. We implore His great mercy for us and are granted forgiveness, but fortunately not in the measure we forgive those who have offended, hurt, or grieved us. Our forgiving of them is typically hesitating and flawed. His forgiveness of us is pristine and perfect. Amazingly, God forgives us without qualifications. His love for us is that pure.

Forgiving others is what we are commanded to do. This is often referred to as burying the hatchet, and Kin Hubbard said it best, "No one ever forgot where they buried the hatchet." We mortals may not be able to forget where it was buried, but we are instructed to forgive and move on with our lives regardless. Some things are hard to forgive, but on the cross, Jesus asked for forgiveness for us and, in particular, for a sinner on a cross next to Him. If He could forgive while in agony, we must at least try to do the same. Again, we are the hesitating and flawed human race He so dearly loves.

The word "regardless" can be used, and maybe necessary, in forgiving others. Hating the sin, yet loving the sinner regardless, is what we are called upon to do.

One true moment of Godly forgiveness came after a mass shooting on October 2, 2006. A gunman broke into an Amish one-room schoolhouse in Nickel Mines, Pennsylvania. He shot ten young girls, killing five and causing severe brain damage to a sixth, before killing himself.

The Amish, only hours after the shooting, went to the killer's family and extended forgiveness. The shooter's widow, parents, and parents-in-law were all comforted by the Amish community with the killer's sobbing father being held in their arms for an hour. Thirty members of the Amish community attended the killer's funeral and his widow was invited to the funeral of one of the victims. As a final act of forgiveness that approaches that of our Savior on the cross, the Amish set up a charitable fund for the family of the shooter. https://en.wikipedia.org/wiki/West_Nickel_Mines_School_shooting

And lead us not into temptation,

We are weak, mortally weak, and satan has spent your lifetime studying your individual weaknesses.

God will not place us into temptation, but our mortal enemy, satan, the prince of the air, has free reign to lead us, tempt us, and torment us as a foretaste to his kingdom below. Our only ally and hope against him is God and His grace, and here we are asking for that divine intervention. We must admit that we often invite satan into our lives through our pride, greed, lust, and arrogance. We make his role in our lives easier through our resentments, envy, and anger.

Corinthians 10:13 provides some reassurance, "No temptation has overtaken you except what is common to mankind. And God is faithful; He will not let you be tempted beyond what you can bear. But when you are tempted, He will also provide a way out so that you can endure it."

It should be noted that temptations and attacks from satan often begin early in the morning and early in the workweek. As a result, we find ourselves in direct contact with others for extended hours where our bruised egos and fragile attitudes can be grated with further irritations. This can lead to resentments, frustrations, and direct confrontations as we go through the rest of our day and workweek.

But deliver us from evil.

We are deeply flawed, especially in our interactions with others. Perhaps the most frightening power of satan is that they are a master of pitting people against each other. The world places us in direct competition with each other for grades, sales, money, etc. This is a ready-made atmosphere for satan to influence our thoughts and the thoughts of those around us. Do others with the same job have a larger salary? Should I tell others of a fact that might be useful to them at my expense? If I help a coworker with their project, will they move ahead of me for a promotion? Pride and fear are a deadly cocktail, especially when alcohol or drugs are added.

The prince of darkness delights in pitting us against each other by simultaneously giving people near each other thoughts that lead to conflicts, irritations, frustrations, and envy. We should know that satan will study us, see our situations, and prod us. Once we are in his clutches, our plight is hopeless, save for God's direct mercy and grace. Deliverance is through His hands alone, and for this, we must pray.

Being a writer, I noticed something significant. At this point, Jesus used two "ands" and a "but" after a request to "Give us this day, our daily bread." These indicate that they are to be taken as a whole, all-inclusive thought.

We are to say, "Give us this day, our daily bread and forgive us our trespasses as we forgive those who trespass against us and lead us not into temptation, but deliver us from evil."

Taken together we see what we need for our day and the power that hell has over us. We must need and know of all of these items daily based on what He instructed us to say.

For thine is the kingdom

For the second time, we are told of the kingdom of heaven, and it is noteworthy that it is prominently brought up twice in such a short prayer. We are again reminded of our predestined home once we shed this mortal vale. Jesus himself has prepared rooms for us and awaits our arrival.

One prominent arrival came when the martyr Stephen, in Acts 7:54-60, saw a vision of Jesus standing, not sitting, at the right hand of the Father as he was being murdered for his faith. We can make the assumption that Jesus was standing in order to greet him. We can well imagine Jesus receiving him with the words, "Well done, good and faithful servant."

And the power

Only at the end of this prayer are we told of His power. At times we are shown God's power in the Old Testament with floods and famine. In the New Testament we see at Jesus' death the tabernacle curtain torn asunder as the earth shook. Today, we can see His power personally as a loved one is cured of cancer, our child is born healthy, and we find a job to support our family. From massive earthquakes to the tiniest personal miracles, His and His alone is the power.

And the glory forever. Amen

Our God, who has all, asks us to repent our sins, accept His Son as our savior, and to glorify Him in our thoughts and deeds. We are told that all honor and glory is His and His alone forever. As an act of devotion, we are to personally glorify Him. John 8:50 tells us, "I am not seeking glory for myself; but there is one who seeks it, and he is the judge." God seeks glory, and He seeks us. Enough to send His Son to die for us.

159

At the end of days, all glory will be shown to be His and His alone forever. As for today, we can glorify Him by serving Him and fanning that spark of Christianity as our way of life.

Serenity Prayer – a Variation

The Serenity Prayer is similarly brief, with most adherents only using the passage, "God grant me the serenity to accept the things I cannot change, Courage to change the things that I can, and wisdom to know the difference," from the original prayer by Reinhold Niebuhr.

This is a call for serenity in our lives where serenity rarely exists. Anxieties, fears, and worries permeate our transitional lives. We find the pressures of the world allow us little serenity, and here we make our plea for comfort for our troubled souls.

In this brief prayer, we do not absolve ourselves of responsibilities, but instead, we freely take on the yoke needed to change what we can. We ask for clarity of mind in knowing what we are charged with and what He will work through. Our confusion must be removed by His grace, comfort, and guidance.

It is noteworthy that millions of twelve-step program members throughout the world have reached for these humble words as their worlds collapsed from alcohol, drugs, gambling, emotions, over eating, and more. In their simplicity we find power, majesty, and a lifeline to God Himself. By the miracles borne from these programs, it seems clear that the inspiration came directly from the Holy Spirit.

I Am There

The prayer "I Am There" was authored by James Dillet Freeman and was taken to the moon by the Apollo 15 astronauts. It was written in response to his desperation for a miracle for his dying wife. In it, we are granted comfort and strength. Through it, we learn more of God's nature and His promises to us. Its haunting poetry never ceases to amaze or inspire me. Next to the Lord's Prayer, it is the prayer that has meant the most to me in my life.

Do you need me?
I am there.

You cannot see Me, yet I am the light you see by.

You cannot hear Me, yet I speak through your voice.

You cannot feel Me, yet I am the power at work in your hands.

I am at work, though you do not understand My ways.

I am at work, though you do not recognize My works.

I am not strange visions. I am not mysteries.

Only in absolute stillness, beyond self, can you know Me as I am, and then but as a feeling and a faith.

Yet I am there. Yet I hear. Yet I answer.

When you need Me, I am there.

Even if you deny Me, I am there.

Even when you feel most alone, I am there.

Even in your fears, I am there.

Even in your pain, I am there.

I am there when you pray and when you do not pray.

I am in you, and you are in Me.

Only in your mind can you feel separate from Me, for only in your mind are the mists of "yours" and "mine."

Yet only with your mind can you know Me and experience Me.

Empty your heart of empty fears.

When you get yourself out of the way, I am there.

You can of yourself do nothing, but I can do all.

And I am in all.

Though you may not see the good, good is there, for I am there.

I am there because I have to be, because I am.

Only in Me does the world have meaning; only out of Me does the world take form; only because of Me does the world go forward.

I am the law on which the movement of the stars and the growth of living cells are founded.

I am the love that is the law's fulfilling. I am assurance. I am peace. I am oneness. I am the law that you can live by. I am the love that you can cling to. I am your assurance. I am your peace. I am one with you. I am.

Though you fail to find Me, I do not fail you.

Though your faith in Me is unsure, My faith in you never wavers, because I know you, because I love you.

Beloved, I am there.

(Used with permission of Unity, unity.org)

Personal Prayers

My friend, Big Bill, of whom I spoke earlier, educated me on the twelve-step Alcoholics Anonymous program. It was founded by Bill W., who was told by a doctor that he was a hopeless alcoholic and would die as such. In abject despair, Bill W. voiced a prayer of desperation, "If there is a God, let Him show Himself! I am ready to do anything, anything." At that moment, the Holy Spirit began to use him to establish the twelve-step program called Alcoholics Anonymous. It seems clear by the miracles borne of these twelve-step programs that they are a twentieth-century incarnation of the Holy Spirit.

My friend told me that a drowning man has no time for a long, fancy prayer. He can only cry out "Help" and that there was just barely enough time to throw in the word "Please." A simple "Please help" can be the prayer we most need to say when we are totally defeated by disease, anger, despair, life, and satan.

Another short prayer he told me, when crushed by the vice of pride, is "Please, rid me of self."

One I use when confronted with exasperating circumstances is "Thy will be done" that I sometimes shorten to simply "Thine." Further, as mentioned before, Psalms enrichens us with, "Be still and know that I am God," which affords us a measure of hope, strength, and tranquility.

It may be important to develop your own personal prayers that you can modify and reinvent as your path continues. Ask for guidance from the Lord in developing them, integrate things that seem important for your personal journey, and experiment with different phrasings. Eventually, you will settle on a prayer path.

Every so often I rewrite my morning prayer, but it always contains consistent elements – a statement of gratitude, a request for help, repudiation of my sins, an appeal for help for family, friends, and those in need, and a petition to help me do the Lord's will this day. My morning prayer needs to be straightforward, but touch on these elements.

One thing I feel drawn on to pray for are those who are spiritually despondent, defeated, or destroyed by satan or the world. I hear of people in pain and include them in my daily prayers by adding the words "and those whom I said I would like to pray for" toward the end. As an example, many years ago, I saw a picture in a magazine of a couple on a beach. There was a look of concern on their faces. The caption explained that they had just realized that they couldn't find their two-year-old child. The child was never found. My prayers have never ended for them and their child.

I typically end my morning prayer with, "I bow before Your wisdom, knowledge, and immeasurable love for us. Regardless of what You choose, let Your will be done today and always, but especially today." We may not know the details of His plans for us today, but we do know that they are based upon His immeasurable love for us. We must bow before His love, guidance, and plans for us each and every day.

Meditation

It was telling that Mother Teresa of Calcutta, when asked about how she prays, said she spent a great deal of time listening. We, too, need to spend some time listening for God's guidance. This can be called meditation - a purposeful, quiet time where we clear our minds, as best we can, of the day's concerns and worries and gain a glimpse of insight of His path for us. We may speak for extended periods to God through our prayers, but we must also allow time for Him to answer, not just in what He sends us during our day, but through our feelings, thoughts, and emotions. The prayer "I Am There" came when James Dillet Freeman was listening. Mother Teresa was guided in what she should do when she listened.

Those of us with rushing minds find this difficult, but we must attempt it and understand that our efforts may improve with time and, interestingly, through a lack of effort. Instead of forcing the issue, serenity is called for. Instead of concentrating on issues, we must concentrate on emptying our minds of issues. We must simply grant God time to answer and guide us.

Puzzle Pieces

Consider the following:
- What do you feel drawn to pray for? Family, friends, those in pain, world peace, the cure of a disease, just getting past a

rough spot in your day, your need to get past an enemy in your life?

- What prayers do you typically say?
- What prayer do you gravitate toward when confused, in pain, or are desperate, or do you simply create your own personal plea?
- If you were to construct a personal prayer, what major points should it concentrate on?
- What does what you pray for say about you?
- What does what you pray for say about your purpose and path in life?

13. Media

One area of our lives to consider is the media that we gravitate toward. We may spend hours on end watching television and movies. We might read books and magazines. The radio and music are a daily staple in many of our lives. Browsing the internet is often a daily routine. And using our cell phones is in a time usage class all by itself. We may deny their influence on us or disparage them as trivial, yet the hours pile up. If we had to write checks for the time we spent with these media, we would have to admit that they are an expensive habit in terms of our time. And time may well be our most pressed resource.

What can we learn from our time spent with these media? It is possible that some of them beckon us with snippets of the path we are meant to tread. They can teach us more about ourselves, our priorities, and our Life Puzzle. If time is a treasure, then where we spend our time says a lot about where our spirits are. Matthew 6:21 phrases it, "For where your treasure is, there will your heart be also."

Songs

Songs may speak to your heart through their lyrics, the meanings you glean from those lyrics, or even the stories behind the songs. Is there something that brings you back to them time and again? I will explain how two have impacted me.

I cannot hear the poignant song, "Amazing Grace," without thinking of the writer and his incredible life path. The Lord selected the captain of a slave-trading ship to work toward the end of slavery in his native England. From the triangle trade to the pulpits where he rallied the nation to end the evil of slavery, John Newton's path was one of complete reversal on the order of Paul's conversion on the way to Damascus. The lyrics, when viewed from this vantage point, become a haunting symbol of the grace bestowed on him by the Holy Spirit.

Newton alternates expressions of the wretchedness of his former life with moments of grace, sweetness, and clarity of sight. In it, he describes his redemption and receiving relief for his uneasy soul. The first section concludes with the evocative "Unending love, Amazing Grace." He undoubtedly was amazed that the Lord could use as shameful a man as he had become for His purposes. Yet often, we see those who had sank the lowest being used by the Holy Spirit and reconstituting themselves for His purposes.

Another favorite song, "It Is Well With My Soul," is poignant and moving when seen from the backdrop of the hymnist Horatio Spafford. At the time he wrote it, all four of his daughters had recently drowned when their ship sank in the Atlantic. Soon thereafter, he sailed to Europe to join his wife who had survived. As his ship passed near where his daughters had died, he was inspired to write the lyrics as a testimony to the serenity placed on his soul by the Holy Spirit. Slow and melancholy, the song evokes tranquility that could only come from Him. The first four lines of the song, conjuring images of water, are telling.

When peace like a river, attendeth my way,
When sorrows like sea billows roll;
Whatever my lot, Thou hast taught me to say,
It is well, it is well, with my soul

We are taught that even in our darkest hour, we can still choose, with His grace, to say it is well with our souls.

Secular songs can also creep into our minds and occasionally they reflect on our daily lives. I have found songs from my youth running in a continuous loop and can't get rid of them. Sometimes, when the lyrics are dissected, they seem to reflect work pressure, wanting to escape a duty, or not having enough time in my life. Other times it is the emotions they conjure up that seems to be the reason for a temporary obsession with a song.

Recently I came to realize that my love of the Christmas song, "Hark the Harold Angels Sing" is based on the blend of lyrics and the music. I now see it as a shout of triumph from mankind and their angel brethren.

Books

Most of us can claim that we were deeply influenced by a specific book, series of books, or author. They may be religious in orientation or strictly secular. All of the following have influenced my path to varying degrees.

The series of short sections that comprise C.S. Lewis' *Mere Christianity* are a hallmark of Christian apologetics. Written with a backdrop of the Battle of Britain during World War II, it provided the British people with a lucid explanation of the principals of Christianity. For readers then and today, it describes how necessary Christianity is to combat evil in our world. We are on battlefield earth where the enemy, satan, has sway over large portions of the population. We are to use our morals, wits, and minds to resist his daily grasps at us. God has provided us with the sacrifice of His only Son, the Holy Spirit, the Bible, His church, and the comradery of fellow Christians as our means to serve in His outnumbered army. We must serve on a specific path He has posited for us.

C.S. Lewis spoke on many topics in this masterpiece and other works, including *The Problem of Pain* and the *Screwtape Letters*. As I have noted, perhaps most interesting of all, he began his path of service to the Lord from the position of a devout atheist who was attempting to disprove Christianity. He ended his life path as one of the most influential Christian writers of the last century. Once again, the Holy Spirit took someone with little to commend themselves for leadership in His service and made use of them for His glory.

Another book that has influenced me is the secular book, *Peter's Quotations: Ideas for Our Times,* by Lawrence J. Peter (Peter, 1977) who also authored *The Peter Principle*. This provides nuggets of wisdom in quotes and instilled in me a love of quotations. Broken down by topics, we are regaled with bits of insight into human nature and, through them, a little deeper into the nature of God. We find that "Doubt isn't the opposite of faith; it is an element of faith." The phrase "We turn toward God only to obtain the impossible" both stings and tells us what many of us have done. A personal favorite mentioned earlier is, "You can tell more about a person by what he says about others than you can by what others say about him." Further, I have often lived the sentiment, "Never put off till tomorrow what you can do the day after tomorrow."

Walden, by Henry David Thoreau, is also something of a favorite, although about halfway through I find myself wishing a blonde would walk through the woods. Thoreau was not one to add romance, action, or excitement, but could still weave a compelling story.

TV and Movies

We commonly spend a great deal of time in front of what is often a vast wasteland known as television. Ernie Kovacs defined it best, "Television: A medium. So called because it's neither rare nor well done." Yet watch the boob tube we do. It is telling of us in how we spend that precious resource, time, with this media.

What is important, possibly, is what we gravitate toward on TV and why. Could our personalities have a predisposition to be drawn to news, documentaries, sitcoms, or dramas? Are there common denominators that help reveal facets of our personalities?

For years I would tell others I didn't need a TV. I had a fireplace. Then I got married.

Since then, my wife and I have a set routine of watching television most evenings with my wife commandeering the remote. I have found that I prefer sports, home improvement, documentaries, and news shows. These seem to indicate I have an inquisitive and methodical, as well as competitive side. You may find pieces to your Life Puzzle in the types of shows you are inclined toward. Or those your spouse keeps switching to.

Some years back, a young man made the national news when he proclaimed that the *Star Wars* movie series was his religion. How serious he was, we can only speculate on, but it was attention grabbing. This can be dismissed outright, but it does speak to one intrinsic trait of the human race, the need to acknowledge our God. Moviegoers did find titbits of superficial wisdom coming from an old, but supposedly wise, Yoda, and to some, this was probably as close to a religious experience as they ever had.

Taking this further, Pascal is often misquoted as saying, "There is a God-shaped vacuum in the heart of every person, and it can never be filled by any created thing." Yet these words are instructive in their own right. The embryonic need to worship our God is ingrained in us by Him at our birth and can grow within us, but it can also be subverted by an atheistic society. The path you were meant to take can be undermined with the cares of the world, sabotaged by satan's demons, or transferred on to a meaningless movie. Regardless, the need to worship our God (and hopefully not Yoda) is very much real, as is the significant opposition to it. How it plays out will be reliant on our decisions, our willingness to reach out to God, and our acceptance of His will for us.

Cell Phones and the Internet

I spend an embarrassing amount of my life on my cell phone, typically browsing the internet or texting with others, and know full well how addictive these beasts can be. Also, my laptop often serves as my gateway to the internet with its avalanche of sites, services, and silliness. Using either, a simple search on a news topic can lead to the loss of an hour from my day as I read the details floating on the internet. Special interest sites, news, music, and games can eliminate much of our free time as we explore the wonders of the web.

However, I have noted something that much of our population has found to be both a truism and is unrecognized by most. Spiders lay very sticky webs for their prey. I think satan has learned from them and is using the twenty-first-century sticky web – the World Wide Web. This web is replete with sticky sites for radicalism, avarice, lust, pride, and all manner of sin. The web site Alexa tracks the number of hits different sites get across the globe, and pornography sites are among the most frequented. Even social media can lend itself to satan's reach. A few years ago, Twitter made worldwide news when it discontinued 125,000 accounts owing to radicalism and concerns about terroristic potential.

The internet has indeed enriched our knowledge base, and commerce, business, and even friendships are intertwined with this modern marvel. Yet it is telling how it impacts us personally and how we use it.

We must decide whether to use internet browsing in an ethical and Christian manner or gravitate to extremists' sites that fan hatred for another soul that God created and dearly loves. Will the World Wide Web serve as chewing gum for our eyes or to let us connect in friendship over social media? What type of sites do we find ourselves drifting toward and, more importantly, how do they warp our interactions with others? All are salient questions we must be able to answer before the Lord.

Puzzle Pieces

Consider the following:

- What media do you primarily use?
- How do you use it?
- Is there any song that has a special meaning to you, and what could that meaning be?
- Do song lyrics keep repeating in your mind? Can you interpret any meaning for you when you hear them?
- Could a song's meaning to you be a puzzle piece for your life?
- Which books have influenced you and the way you think?
- How has their influence played out in your life?
- Could a book's message to you be a puzzle piece for your life?
- Are there any specific types of TV shows or movies that dominate your viewing? What does that say about you?
- What are the five internet sites you most frequent and what will they tell Jesus about you when you meet Him?
- How has the internet impacted your thoughts? Do those thoughts impact your life? Is it a Christian impact?
- Where does your cell phone lead you? Does that have an impact on your path?

14. Your Opposition

On our path, we will face opposition from society, personal enemies, time, our inherent weaknesses, and satan. God is very aware of our plight. He made us the faltering human race and loves us in spite of our sins and weaknesses. His love for us is similar to that of a father for a child that is trying to walk, but needs assistance just to stand.

Our greatest concern is satan. Relentlessly he is dedicated to preventing you from knowing your path, frustrating your daily life, confusing your mind, and destroying your soul. Your God-decreed path to joy, fulfillment, and happiness will be frustrated by him, and you may even be prevented from knowing of these riches.

Other opponents come from being worn down by life, addictions, emotional turmoil, society, etc. All may be encountered. All can be overcome with grace from Him.

Our Weaknesses

You will stumble from your weaknesses, but you may gain strength from them in some regards as God assists you in your struggles. You might even overcome them with God's grace. Some overcome fears such as of public speaking, social situations, or heights. With God's strength, Moses became the leader he could not have imagined he would be. Alcoholics Anonymous members have reclaimed much of their lives through the intervention of the Holy Spirit. The lists are many, and God's miracles are shown consistently in history.

Still again, these weaknesses may indicate where God does not want you to venture. They may even be ingrained biochemically in you. Some of us are physically weak; others are born athletes. Some of us would flail in a career based on mathematics; others would thrive. Some of us are models of organization; some are at a loss for even basic time management skills.

So how can you tell if specific weaknesses are meant to be overcome or if they are meant to be over you? You may be placed in a position where you are required to overcome them, and an ability you previously did not have may appear. The Holy Spirit may well provide you with a new ability, and the path may be arduous or one of relative ease. Regardless, it is often time-consuming. You may find a nascent interest leading to a path to develop certain skills, which, in turn, leads to an ability.

Examples of overcoming weaknesses are found throughout history. Bill W., with the help of the Holy Spirit, led many out of addictions. John Newton led efforts to end slavery after his years as a slave ship captain.

Of more recent years, Stephen Hawking, possibly the greatest physicist of our era, lived decades within a body ruined by amyotrophic lateral scierosis (ALS). The Academy Award-winning actress, author, and activist Marlee Matlin became deaf at 18 months. Cornel Hrisca-Munn was born so deformed that his birth mother screamed in horror, and the doctor gave him days to live. Without forearms and an amputated leg, he won a national drumming competition at the age of fourteen.

Still, many are not given the ability to overcome their weaknesses. Their paths are to be different. Their paths are to be unique. Their paths are to be God's paths for them.

No remedy to a weakness may emerge, and you may be left with an inability to work well with numbers, lead people, handle finances, or work with computers. An acceptance, bound on the virtue of humility, may be called for as we accept His limitations and the boundaries set for us.

"Know thyself," counseled Willy Shakespeare, and we must attempt to do so. Earlier in this book, a searching inventory of your traits, interests, abilities, and weaknesses formed the puzzle border that is you. Certain talents may reside outside of this framework. Yet unnoticed elements may be contained within this boundary. Your attempts to develop math skills may or may not be fruitful, leadership skills may or may not emerge, a mechanical aptitude may or may not materialize, but attempt you can and then leave the results in God's hands. What is important is the attempt and learning from the results you are handed. You will have learned more about His path and plans for you in doing so.

What Wears You Down

What will wear you down and prevent you from finding and working your path is typically the mundane routines in life. You may be a seed growing among thorn bushes choked by the worries of the world. Daily concerns, repetitive burdens, and the mosquito bites of life will wear you down. Time that you could use to work on your path will evaporate. The perceived enormity of problems in achieving your goals will seem insurmountable. You will be in the position of trying to eat an elephant and not realize you eat it one bite at a time. An attitude and a determination are called for. You do not complete a four-year college degree in four weeks, you do not reach a twentieth wedding anniversary in twenty days, and you do not raise children to adulthood in a year, although it may feel that way.

A steady determination, combined with God's grace, is necessary. We will be ground down at times, but, like grist for our spiritual mill, that determination alone will be a great strength. We must continue on our path regardless and relentlessly. The ancient adage is true - a journey of a thousand miles is taken a single step at a time.

Proverbs 4:16 tells us we can receive comfort when we feel worn down, "Let us then approach God's throne of grace with confidence, so that we may receive mercy and find grace to help us in our time of need." And we will need His mercy, especially when raising children seems a merciless task.

Time

Time is that stuff that matters. God knows it, satan knows it, and even we sometimes know it. A rich man who gives you a gift is kind, but the cost means little to them. A busy person who gives you their time is very kind and cares enough about you to give you what costs them much. Think of your mother and father. If you are a mother or father, you may be nodding your head at this moment.

I was told when I first went to college that misuse of time is the greatest problem of new students. I handled time well, more out of fear of failing, but I saw it squandered by many.

Among the things satan steals from us is time. I've always thought it interesting that the person who wants to live forever often doesn't know what to do with themselves on a Sunday afternoon. We are unable to find time when it is needed, yet later find ourselves killing time the same day. Often the equation doesn't balance, and we are at a loss for time when it is most required. Time pressures come down on us, and we can react with anger, frustration, fear, and remorse. The devil can nicely find an opening through this emotional upheaval.

Time is often squandered through sin. Sin is a phenomenal robber of time, as well as money. Hours can easily be lost indulging in the vices. Alcohol wastes weekends, we lose evenings involved in adultery, and days and lives are lost to drug abuse. Many have found that their vices have led to their "doing time" in prison. Sin is an expensive proposition in terms of time and money, as well as to the damage they inflict on jobs, families, friends, and souls. Not only do they take clock time in the commission, but we then waste time and money worrying about their consequences and attempting to cover our tracks. As though we could cover our tracks before God. Sometimes it appears we get away with things, sometimes we obviously do not, and sometimes we get a good scare. A good scare is always better than good advice. But in the end, our time, money, and souls are lost.

Diligence is required in our use of time. This is a constant and earnest effort to accomplish what is needed in our lives and in serving our Lord. We must use our time wisely and, more specifically, use it to grow in our faith continuously. Stagnation or neglect leads to decay in what we are and what we are meant to be. We must strive forward on our path with diligence. Continuous growth in Christ is the ruination of satan's plans for us.

Addictions

Addictions are a predictable part of most lives. Although often innocuous, it may be possible for them to grow into vices that inflict pain on our loved ones and us. We must know of our addictions and be diligent in observing their effects on us and our path. Common addictions include sugar, TV, the internet, cell phones, computer games, coffee, food, sports, spending money, negative thoughts, etc. These are known equally well to God and satan, and occasionally they spiral out of control.

Addictions with more significant consequences include anger, pride, lying, pornography, alcohol, gambling, drugs, etc. These can have a more intense and quicker impact on our lives. It seems that we all know of people who succumbed to these addictions and took parts of the lives of others down with them. Treatments vary in effectiveness and may depend less of self-will than on surrender to God. The twelve-step programs tell adherents to consider reliance on self-will as a liability and surrender of their situation to their "Higher Power" as a strength. The acceptance of one's condition and the determination to initiate and remain in treatment may be the greatest hope for some who are deeply afflicted.

A small but seemingly harmless vice can always become a debilitating addiction. There seems to be an addictive type of personality that will take an innocent, or not so innocent, vice and have it spiral out of control.

One such addict I learned of from a dear friend was the co-owner of a car dealership she inherited from her father. Over time she became addicted to astrology. She easily found someone to take her money and give her what was called astrological guidance. One day she was told to sell her part of the dealership now, not tomorrow, not this afternoon, but now. By week's end, she had signed the papers and was then told to move to a small town in a different time zone. In the next few years, she was ordered to move several more times to small towns she had never heard of. The last I heard about her was that she had become fanatical on her two dogs. You were not allowed to meet them until you had read a book on their breed. She dedicated her life to them to the point where all movies shown in her house were for the viewing pleasure of the dogs. A small interest in astrology had led to a life based on the whims of their astrologer and further debilitating behaviors.

A previously uncommon, but highly toxic, addiction is the drug of political extremism. It is now found more frequently in western democracies, but less so in totalitarian nations like Russia, China, and some third-world nations where freedom of thought is deeply constrained. A news article, "Politics is a Jealous God," has made the disturbing, and possibly entirely accurate, claim of a direct link between the de-Christianization of America and the parallel rise in political tribalism.   https://frenchpress.thedispatch.com/p/politics-is-a-jealous-god?utm_campaign=post&utm_medium=web&utm_source=email

Politics has emerged as a de facto competing religious force with enmity as its creed. Political hate and fear are being seized with an absolute religious zeal. Christ's teachings and His ultimate sacrifice for all mankind have no place in many minds when politics is at the fore. Some demand that hatred of others who think differently, similar to George Orwell's *1984* dystopian term "thoughtcrime," is what is needed, not the love and compassion that came to us 2,000 years ago.

The article makes a convincing argument that the two American cultural phenomena - the increase in America's negative political polarization and the decline in American religious identification are linked and mutually self-reinforcing. These two antithetical movements are expected to continue and reinforce each other in snowballing effects. The Christian youth of today may realize they are a distinct minority in our nation, but over the next few decades, they may well see their numbers decline even more. These young Christian men and women could easily live to see historic juxtaposition levels between growing political movements and a retreating religious realm. The future of Christianity and its place in society will rely on this new generation and their level of courage.

Enemies

You will often find that there are those in your life who wish you ill. They may feel they have been first abused by you, or they may be acting out of pride, wrath, greed, or envy. Frequently they may feel it is "fun" to belittle, harm, and abuse others. They can be avoided at times, ignored at times, or confronted at times. Courage will be needed for all three.

At times you will receive unjust harm because of them. God knows of it, and you can ask for comfort from the Holy Spirit. Serenity may enter you, but it may not. In the worst case, satan may influence you, if you allow him to, and you will strike back in revenge.

That satan has worked on the other person for an extended period may be apparent or strangely absent. Their personality may be an indicator.

We must know that satan delights in working on the emotions of people in close proximity, physically or emotionally, giving each thoughts to conflict with the other. A snowball effect is his hope and long-term animosity his goal. He hopes we will obsess on conflicts he arranged for and have flashbacks to earlier slights and confrontations. The devil knows human fear and anger well. The overflow from these can spill over to other relationships at home or the office. It is often extremely difficult to "let go and let God" and allow Him to handle things.

The devil knows that pain caused by others is what we will very frequently react to, emotionally and physically. Marcel Proust nailed it with, "To wisdom and goodness we only make promises. Pain we obey." It doesn't matter if World War III is going on outside, if you have a toothache you will go out and find a dentist. If you have pain caused by a coworker, you may also go out of your way to find a way to get back at them. We are in emotional pain and want to lash back instead of ignoring or swallowing it - or praying for them.

These situations are designed to take you off your path toward God. The jigsaw puzzle pieces of your life will be pulled up and jumbled up from pain and anger.

You may be in such a situation to learn a lesson from God on strength, reliance on Him, or to stand up for decency and Christian behavior. You may learn more about yourself for going through it. Growth frequently comes at the cost of pain.

Remaining resolute on your path, confronting enemies when required, and sidestepping them when advisable may be the best you can do. You might even consider the Chinese proverb, "If thine enemy wrong thee, buy each of his children a drum."

However, the Bible guides us much better in Matthew 18:15-17 whereby we tell them of their wrong. If they refuse to take blame or laugh at you then having others who confront them with you is advised. Then your church family can be employed to show them their wrong. Three increasingly formidable attempts are advised, after which they need to be purged from your life as possible. Circumstances may determine this extent.

Prayer for them and all, including yourself, who were affected by the pain they inflicted, must be employed and leaned on. The Holy Spirit will grant you both strength and common sense regarding the other person. You must use both, not one.

You may reach a type of accord with these others and "bury the hatchet." This may help, but things rarely revert to the way they were before an incident. As quoted earlier, "No one ever forgot where they buried the hatchet." The Holy Spirit, time, prayer, and the comfort of others are the great healers.

Possession by satan

In the 1960s, the movie *The Exorcist* showed a small girl possessed by the devil, and America was terrorized. People placed crucifixes over their beds, and polls asked people if they knew of anyone who had been possessed, with many responding that they did.

What was less known was that the actual events the movie was based on were even more terrifying.

A young boy, who had been introduced to the Ouija board by a spiritualist aunt, became possessed by demonic entities. Soon after the aunt's death, the family experienced strange noises, furniture moving on its own accord, and objects flying when the boy was near. The words "evil" and "hell" appeared on the boy's body, and the mother reported seeing the word "Louis" on the boy's chest. The family took this as a call to move to St. Louis to be with family, and there, at the Catholic Jesuit College of St. Louis University and the Alexian Brothers Hospital, the thirteen-year-old boy underwent an actual exorcism. The exorcism took many days and was marked by violent outbursts as the boy viciously fought against the priests performing the ritual.

In the end, a voice came out of the boy announcing they were the archangel Michael and that they were expelling satan. (Tomlinson, 2013) (Lvcifer, 2011) The child recovered completely from the ordeal.

Possession, from what we can tell in the Bible, was common in the ancient world. Jesus cast out demons frequently and gave his disciples the power to do so as well. From what little we know; demons seem to work in packs. The man possessed by "legion" was cured by Jesus. The exorcism of the boy in St. Louis was of multiple demons. Further, there seem to be different types of demons. Mark 9:29 tells us, "He replied, 'This kind can come out only by prayer.'"

In his excellent study on evil, *People of the Lie*, M. Scott Peck, M.D., begins with the words, "This is a dangerous book." It is very much a dangerous and frightening book covering human evil, possession, and satan. Peck covers multiple cases of viciously evil things that people have both perpetrated and have fallen victim to. Perhaps most disturbing were two instances of satanic possession he encountered. As part of an exorcism team, he testified to the satanic transfiguration of one such victim. A facial expression he could only describe as satanic came upon the individual. He testified that their body suddenly resembled a writhing snake as it attempted to attack the team members. Both exorcisms were successful, and the victims were able to recover their lives (Peck, 1983).

Peck went on to theorize that satan's true power lay in human belief in its lies. He further speculated that satan is a retreating enemy who has long since lost the war. I read the daily news. I am not as optimistic.

Possession seems to have been a common, though terrifying occurrence in Biblical times. Yet today possession seems very rare. The causes for this change are purely speculative, but Christ's triumph from the tomb, the single greatest event in the history of mankind, may have changed the world in ways we do not know.

Large-scale possessions by demons may have ended at that time. We will never know for certain.

The devil is a Gentleman

A quote I disagree with, but is instructive nevertheless, is, "The devil is a gentleman who never goes where he is not welcome," by John A. Lincoln. Proverbs 11:27 phrases the sentiment similarly, "Whoever seeks good finds favor, but evil comes to one who searches for it." Further, Job's friend, Eliphaz the Temanite noted in Job 4:8, "As I have observed, those who plow evil and those who sow trouble reap it."

We often welcome satan into our lives, claiming we can belittle someone for fun, are sophisticated enough to indulge in some high-class pornography, or that a few drunken episodes are clearly needed for the pressure we are under. Regardless, we invite evil into our lives.

A trip to Las Vegas seems fun until you realize Las Vegas is the place that the people from Sodom and Gomorrah would have gone to for the weekend to have a wild time.

179

Remember that the devil is a devouring lion. Years ago, there was a story of a man in South Africa who was trying to set a world record. He was attempting to live the longest in a glass cage with some of the deadliest snakes on earth. I remember thinking he was a blithering idiot. We, too, can be blithering idiots by willingly entering into situations where we can be tempted by the snake. With that "harmless" third drink, a small lie for "fun," or seeing what can be found on the internet, we invite the "gentleman" in.

God is aware of our weaknesses, as is satan. In fact, satan is fascinated enough to study ours in particular, whereas God wants to overlook them. Each weak link in our armor is noted. Our idiosyncrasies and quirks are known well. A tiny crack is all satan asks for.

Do not make the mistake of thinking satan is working on us individually. As noted earlier, he often seems to work on us in pairs and small groups, knowing it can be much more effective. The devil can prod a spouse to be a bit sarcastic toward something we did, an acquaintance can insinuate they could have done something better, or a coworker might imply that they would be a better choice for our job. Each would suffice for an opening. These can lead to thoughts placed in our minds to escalate the issue, which leads to greater intensification, hostility, and hard feelings. The spear is thrown down, and a month from now we will remember the what's, when's, and where's. It will never cross our minds that it may be satan's prodding. Long term patterns and resentments serve him well, and no one is better at building them.

Viciously he works on our thoughts and emotions in the present. The devil reminds us of things that hurt us in our past. And satan works on our pride for things in the future.

In C.S. Lewis' masterpiece *The Screwtape Letters*, Screwtape and other demons were cannibals that ate upon brethren who failed their assignments to gain human souls. Human souls also were likewise devoured with eagerness. (I will add that a very fine argument can be made that many humans are cannibals of other souls during their brief lives on earth.) How a soul was killed made no difference to these evil creatures, but human emotions and extremism seemed to add spice to their human cuisine.

A Single Cancer Cell

One question that should be asked is what hurts satan. A quote by C.S. Lewis is instructive, "Above all else, the devil cannot stand to be mocked." We are told satan became satan and was cast into hell because of pride. Being mocked is the antithesis of pride.

When I decided to write this book, I decided not to capitalize the name "satan." My spellchecker keeps flagging the name despite my changes to the proofing tool. I want to make a statement on how small satan actually is. I take my queue once again from C.S. Lewis, who, in *The Great Divorce*, describes a bus ride from heaven to hell and determines that hell is a minuscule place compared to the immensity of heaven. Interestingly, given a choice between spending eternity in either place, most people on the bus select hell. It is the life they have always known, and they fear change.

We may see satan and hell as small, but phenomenally dangerous. He is a single cancer cell that wants only to grow inside you. All you need do is feed him.

Radicalism

Arguably, the internet has become the most important tool of the past two decades. But what type of tool is it?

We need to see this marvel as less of a personal tool to move small data files around than an earthquake that can move civilizations around. It truly seems to have made a seismic shift in society.

As mentioned earlier, the internet has led to a fundamental and disturbing shift in what is now called "news." Many people go to sites for confirmation of a very narrow set of beliefs. They go for affirmation for a small, restricted degree of ideas. They avoid information from the full range of ideas, knowledge, and perspectives available.

And to what end? Inbreeding and radicalization are now being seen in our society as an inevitable result. Internet "news" sites, and many radio and television shows, have become echo chambers for progressively fanatical hysteria. The leaders of these sites seem to compete to become even more extreme than their peers. The impact on society is akin to that fourth martini — the drinker doesn't care. Just shut up and give me another. Damn the price!

Hearing different ideas and perspectives requires people to think critically on what is presented — an action that today irritates many, inflames some, and infuriates a few. Analytical thought and reflection are now efforts that are being avoided by many, if not most.

Decades ago, the vast majority of Americans classified themselves as moderates. They would listen to other people and ideas that conflicted with their mindset. Civil discourse was accepted, encouraged, and customarily provided by the media of that era. Independent, critical thought was considered the God-bestowed right of everyman, and no one was allowed to wrest that right from us.

Today we see that moderate majority dwindling. Civil discourse is attacked by the extremes and in increasingly angered rhetoric. Moderation in thought is beginning to be seen as a greater danger than those who are radically opposed to our positions.

Earlier in this book, the growth of radicalized political movements and the co-joined diminishing ranks of Christians was discussed. These seem linked and mutually reinforcing, but in actuality, they are just visual reflections in a cloudy mirror. These are the outward, fevered symptoms of the underlying cancer.

Extremist movements are highly emotional, exciting in an odd sense, fodder for historian debates a century hence, and, in what will be the final analysis of mankind, unimportant.

What will be important is whether our actions, in our pitiful few years on earth, follow Christ's example when He allowed us to touch His cloak, ate with tax collectors and sinners, and showed us honor and dignity as verbal abuse led to death by torture.

Will our actions and words echo His and serve to place our souls (our only link to God and eternity) on His path for us? Or will our actions and words serve the one who has nothing but scorn for politics, money, fame, or any other human ailment? The devouring lion has never forgotten that we, not he, were made in God's image. Does satan care who were political rulers and non-rulers two-thousand years ago? Will satan care a thousand years from today who won any election held this year? Of course he won't, and he may very well exist for eternity.

Will, at the end of your short lifespan, satan care if your fanaticism caused him to own your soul for eternity? Of course he will, and he may very well exist for eternity.

In the current day, we seem to have progressively myopic eyesight and find ourselves begging for blindness. There are two skyscrapers that are being built in our society that are too huge for most to see. We simply do not see two fast-growing forests for the tree branch we are sitting in.

The first, and more minor, of these structures is that only a handful of left wing and right wing leaders determine what their followers are allowed to believe. The worst thing one of their disciples can do is question what these few leaders order them to think. Independent thought by any follower is traitorous to the point of Judas himself. They are to listen and agree in goose-step. Independent thought and personally deciding what to believe has been a recognized danger to those in power since Biblical times. Tolerance for dissent is waning and at a snowballing pace. Independent, critical thought is anathema to these controllers.

The second superstructure is far eviler. What is overlooked is satan's roll in this. Do you really think the devil actually cares about political movements? He knows humans die in roughly eighty years and then can be seized by his kingdom below. The devil has existed since the God created him near or before the beginning of time. Clearly, satan has scorn for lives that exist less than a second on his timescale. As noted, we were created in God's image, not him, and he never forgot it. We will be prodded by him to join these extremes where he knows we will hate, attack, and inflict evil upon others that God Himself has created.

A fundamental goal of satan is to have us forget that we live our pitifully few years on a live battlefield between God and him. The length of our lives is almost nonexistent when viewed by these two combatants, but at the end of our lifespans, we will forfeit our souls to one or the other. To have us hate our neighbor because of their political beliefs or race is an unbelievable gift to satan. The more radical we become, the more we detest our fellow man, and the more rage we direct against another God-created soul because of their race, politics, or other illusion of difference, the more we build satan's claim on our soul. And worse, the more bewildered is our heartbroken God.

183

Today we find that many websites and locations on Facebook, Twitter, Instagram, and the rest are Petri dishes for radicalization. Nourishing these are foreign actors, including Russia's GRU (military intelligence branch) and their Chinese, North Korean, and Iranian counterparts, with more most assuredly coming. Domestic groups across the belief spectrum may spew even more venom. These have been able to warp American society by pushing political, societal, and other extremes, uncaring for results other than a more divided American society. Their service, knowingly or otherwise, to satan's specific plans for your individual soul is respected by him. In the afterlife, we may well be told that these organizations and websites are among the few that satan actually politely bowed to out of respect.

The further the gauge needle of a radio, television, or internet site pulls into the red indicating bitterness, loathing, prejudice, and abhorrence toward imagined human differences, the closer the needle moves in the direction of hell.

However, this is a very short-term situation, as satan almost always employs. It will only impact you for as long as you live. But what happens that minute after a doctor signs your death certificate? There is a measurement, of sorts, that is as obvious as it is ignored.

That measurement is, after both you and that other person you detest for whatever reason, die, will your differences during your past life make any difference on what you will think of them in the afterlife (let alone what God thinks of both of you)? After we all achieve death, will that person's political affiliation, ethnic origin, religious beliefs, sexual orientation, race, developmental disability, and the thousand other supposed differences between you and them matter? Simply put, will you continue your hatred of them once both of you exist only as souls in heaven?

Will you retain any of your supposed superior traits when to dust you will return? Will they bring to the afterlife the political beliefs, race, sexual practices, intelligence levels, etc., that assured you of their inferiority to you? Both you and they will be dead and exist in that afterlife much, much longer than our four score in this stumbling, bumbling human life. It is there we will live for eternity, and we will see even the longest life spans on earth as barely registering.

Although I identify with the religious right, I deliberately have eight news apps across the social spectrum on my cell phone and access them frequently. I will not surrender my independent, Christian judgments to the extremist "news" sources and leaders who live on pride and arrogance toward both their followers or their opposite fanatics. The calls of political extremes, racial radicals, or angry social groups are often the dog whistle of satan.

At a far more critical level, I attempt to hold respect, civility, consideration, and cordiality to all whom God Himself has bestowed souls to. If He gave His only Son to be tortured for the person I diametrically disagree on politics with, then I can act in a decent manner toward them.

We are God's beloved children. We are to sit up straight and act like it, not like moody, spoiled children who do not want to listen to someone we disagree with or eat our vegetables. Being God's children means we have responsibilities we absolutely will not like. Regardless, we are to act in an appropriate manner. His Son showed us what a life of honor, decency, dignity, modesty, and propriety is like. We must attempt to do the same.

I also know that in acting in a decent manner toward others I disagree with or even dislike, I earn satan's deeper personal hatred of me – and I am grateful to God for that.

Puzzle Pieces

Consider the following:

- What weaknesses do you have in finding your God-decreed path in life?
- What are the daily things that seem to wear you down?
- That you will have enemies in life is undeniable. How do you handle them, and what will you do in the future regarding them?
- What addictions do you find yourself gravitating toward, and how significant are their influences?
- Can a fellow Christian be of a different political persuasion, Christian denomination, racial group, ethnic group, gender, or somehow significantly different from what you call a Christian? How far will you allow them to be different than

your definition of a Christian before they are not considered a soul in God's eyes?

- In what ways do you allow satan a toehold into your life?
- What weaknesses does satan attempt to exploit in you?
- In the coming week, where could satan influence you or those near you?
- Is time usage a significant issue in your life, and how does that impact your life path?
- Does political radicalization appeal, even slightly to you? Can it cripple your service to Jesus?
- Is your race, culture, or nationality a factor in your self-definition of yourself? Does God care?

15. Your Future

Christianity is a way of life, and that way of life involves stewardship of the gifts we have been given. From Adam through today, we are called upon to be guardians of our traits, interests, abilities, and relationships, and that is only a start. Our society needs us to be good stewards of our churches, schools, government, organizations we belong to, and much more.

Do you feel overwhelmed? That is a feeling, not a reality. We are Christians, we are not small men!

To repeat, 1 Peter 4:10 tells us, "Each of you should use whatever gift you have received to serve others, as faithful stewards of God's grace in its various forms." You have been given a multitude of gifts and been charged with Christianity as a way of life. The pieces of your Life Puzzle may still be jumbled, but the outside edge has been built. Further, we have portions of our puzzle constructed based on what we have learned about ourselves at critical junctions, our interactions with others, our education, work, finances, media choices, etc. Pieces have been locked together based on what our past experiences have been and the promises of what we are to become.

We are to take the gifts God has given us, accept them, give thanks, and then we must use them. We are accountable for our lives and how we use His gifts to us. They are not for regifting. Our accountability groups would include our marriages, church family, friendships, work, school, etc. We were not given talents to be left on a serving tray; they were meant to serve Him.

Never forget - we are Christians, we are not small men!

Our Starting Point

So how might you start your path at this particular point in your life? You may find that first baby step to be the hardest and most confusing of all steps, but you are in good company.

Imagine that you were to suddenly find yourself in heaven standing next to the great saints of biblical and more recent times, you might expect them to give you a confused look like you were an unordered side dish at a restaurant. But be fully aware that those saints were probably unordered side dishes at one time themselves. Others would have looked at them, wondering what they were doing there as well.

In Romans 7:15, Paul writes, "I do not understand what I do. For what I want to do, I do not do, but what I hate I do." Surprising words from a man who wrote much of the New Testament.

We are in the same boat and are liable to feel as shipwrecked as he was. Sins and vice are our shipboard companions. We neglect our true path and are often clueless as to even what it is. So, what did these saints do about their shipwrecks? They repented their sins, accepted Jesus as their savior, and came to the Lord by beginning their paths as shown them by the Holy Spirit.

Simply put, they lived differently. They lived Christianity as a way of life. We can begin to do the same. And that will begin connecting chunks of linked pieces together inside our puzzle outline. Daily tasks can be undertaken this very hour with gladness of heart, instead of irritation. Arrange to play a movie that your parents, siblings, and children would all like for a family evening tonight. Quality work at the office can replace doing enough work to get by. Friendships can be strengthened with a phone call. Encouragement and help can be given to fellow students. Relationships can be mended after neglect has left them in tatters.

Once we have started attempting to live Christianity as a way of life, we have launched our second boat. The boat that has been sent to rescue us from our shipwrecked lives. This boat will take us on the path to our "true north," our sacred home with Him. Now we come to Him and will sail as navigated by Him.

How do we come to the Lord? Often, we don't come out of altruistic motives; often, we come out of pain. The twelve-step programs, like Alcoholics Anonymous, were founded on pain. No one ever came through their doors because things were going well in their lives. Other times we come to God not out of pain, but out of confusion and sadness about our lives. At still other times, we come because we feel an odd pulling toward Christians who seem much happier than we are. Regardless of what spurs us to actively search for Him and His comfort, we soon realize that God accepts us where we are and for what we are. Remember, remember, remember that Jesus said he came for the sick, not for the healthy, and we are all at least in the admitting ward. He knows we are sick. He made us. He knows our pain and sins and accepts us exactly as we are. But at any stage of health or sickness, we are called to walk in His path and become overseers of our paths.

Do not be unduly distressed by the brokenness of mankind or of yourself. History and lives are composed of brokenness, mending, and redemption. We repair the world and we repair ourselves through His grace, living deliberately with Christianity as a way of life, the guidance of the Holy Spirit, and daily battling satan in our lives and society.

We have been developing self-awareness of our abilities and responsibilities. We have seen the good, the bad, the ugly, and the beautiful in our lives. We are more aware of our needs and the need that God has for us. He very much needs us to fulfill what He preordained us to do. We are irreplaceable in His eyes and necessary for the world He wants.

At the very moment you read this sentence, know beyond all doubt that you are valuable and loved by God Himself.

Our Life Puzzle is being assembled, although with gaping holes that represent our future. Additional pieces will be provided by critical junctions, our fellow man, turmoil, triumphs, and the Holy Spirit at their appointed hours. As you learn from your past, it is not too early to plan parts of your future. What is more, you can begin to practice for them.

Practicing our Future

Yes, you can practice your future. Part of stewardship is planning for the future, and many major future decisions can be made and practiced in advance. We can plan and practice ahead what we will say and do as that future arises. A kicker does not go out onto the field without hundreds of practice kicks, a speaker does not deliver a major address without numerous rehearsals, an actor learns their lines by heart before walking up to the camera, and a woodworker spends hundreds of hours working in their craft before building fine pieces of furniture.

You can begin to assess possibilities for your future and what they might entail. You can take an online college class or read material in a work field or personal interest you feel called toward. You can plan in advance how you will handle a possible death in the family. The potential loss of a job can be evaluated for options for your family.

Smaller and more intimate issues can be equally addressed. You can plan ahead for how you will handle sexual advances. Your response to financial pressures from your spouse can be considered and decided upon beforehand. How to handle family holiday pressures can be discussed and decided upon early. How to deal with the possibility of your child making poor choices in friends can be thought of in advance. In doing these things proactively, we become better stewards of our lives. These puzzle pieces will be assembled and in place when we need them.

Changes in Your Life

Are you being called upon to make significant changes in your life? Possibly. Do you have the time, money, and discipline to make these major changes? Me neither.

We are overloaded with commitments, promises, and work. There is information overload and obligation overkill. And yet we clearly have poverty with time and money.

The changes you may decide to make in yourself, based on what you deduce as God's probable path for you, do not have to be large. Instead, they may be minor alterations that can grow all out of proportion as the Holy Spirit works on them. Little is much when God is involved.

The "Butterfly Effect" is the effect that small, seemingly inconsequential actions can have on larger actions later. It was coined in computer meteorological research where it was shown that a trivial action could have an impact on large weather patterns later in another part of the world. Small changes in your attitudes, behaviors, and actions today can impact the larger you of the future. A college course in an area you know little of can result two years later in a career change. The extra time you spend with a fellow church member can lead to a lifelong friendship. That book you read on the plane, thinking it would be good for you, may lead to a noticeably better you in relationships. Playing audio recordings of the Bible as you drive to work may very well lead you down your Christian path better.

In Malcolm Gladwell's influential book, *The Tipping Point*, he spoke of how small actions can result in major movements in culture and society. The influence of a few select types of people and minor actions, changes, or influences can launch a social movement, popular marketing campaign, or cultural shift.

Small, simple changes you make in your current life today may well mimic this pattern and result in powerful changes in your future life, abilities, and capabilities. Small corrections today may well alter the trajectory of your future. As mentioned before, you will move foothills in your life, and the mountains will know of it.

An old story is instructive on how a small change in attitude can impact your behavior so that it is noticed by all. In a village in India, a man was sitting meditating while Sufi whirling dervishes were spinning and shrieking just a few feet away. When his family, friends, and others asked how he could remain so calm, he replied, "I just decided to let them whirl." In a whirling, shrieking world, you can make a decision to be a calm example of what the Holy Spirit can do as you live Christianity as your way of life.

In his similarly excellent book, *Blink*, Malcolm Gladwell describes how we size up situations, as well as people, in the blink of an eye. He champions the idea that we can appraise what is important within a very narrow timeframe. Spontaneous judgments are often as good as, if not superior to, carefully planned decisions. He makes a convincing argument that taking a long, laborious time to consider all alternatives typically results in analysis paralysis and poorer choices.

In determining your path, your "gut" feelings may need to be a critical and significant factor. Understanding your current life situation might be a quick glance at your emotional state away. Perceiving God's intent for you over the coming year may need you to acknowledge intuitive feelings that may be eating at you.

Puzzle Pieces

How will you serve as a better guardian of the many facets of your life? What small, starting steps can you take that will have some impact on the following list of slices of life? Do not worry if your actions seem inconsequential at first. Persistent, small steps lead to running the marathon that your life path will resemble.

Consider the following:

- Attitude. Can you become less frustrated by your children and accept that they are acting for what they are – children? Can you accept that most customers are reasonably well mannered toward you? Do you really need to impress others when out in public? What attitudes can be changed in your life?
- Family. What is a step you can take to bring your family closer? A picnic this weekend? Renting a movie that brings up good memories? Decorating the house together for an upcoming holiday?
- Spouse. What steps can you take to make your spouse feel more appreciated? A foot massage? Buying them their favorite flower? Taking them to the high school basketball game? A weekend of their favorite meals?
- Friendships. A call to a friend who is looking for a job? Breakfast on Saturday at McDonalds? Helping them with a yard sale?
- Money. Checking out a Dave Ramsey book from the library? Planning out a clothing budget for the coming month? Carpooling to save on gas? Using folders to collect receipts for taxes?
- Education. Reading a book that you think would be good for you? Watching a documentary on a topic you think might be interesting? Exploring online a subject that might be useful at work?
- Work. Being proactive in work that is coming down the pipe? Being caught up reading and organizing your emails? Arriving fifteen minutes early to organize your day's work?

- Health. Arranging for that dental exam you need? A walk over the weekend with all family members? Eating healthy at a restaurant? Going to bed early to get a full eight hours of sleep?
- Home. Organizing the garage? Using the clothes hamper instead of the floor? Eating items in the back of the refrigerator and pantry for a week before they expire?
- Time. Combining multiple trips in the car into one? Skipping the evening television shows? Working your lunch hour so as to leave work early?
- Church. Serving as a greeter? Bringing snacks to a function? Volunteering for a committee? Shaking hands with a new person who seems lost?
- In Public. Picking up litter? Using a grocery cart left in the parking lot? Allowing another driver to enter into your lane?
- Social Groups. Serving on a committee? Volunteering to be an officer? Researching online a social group that might be good for both you and for them?

16. Your Path

Now, you have an amalgam of what you are and what you can become. You have an idea as to your personality traits, abilities, and weaknesses. You know better your childhood proclivities, your innate interests, what you can thrive at in work and school, and what you crash and burn doing.

You now better recognize the influence of people God has placed in your life, seen critical junctions meant to instruct you, and know the media you respond to. You've seen how money affects you, the social groups you favor, and the impact of virtues and vices in your life. Health and dreams have been considered, as have the prayers you gravitate toward. You have grasped how His church and church family have impacted you. You better understand satan's hatred of you and the tactics he uses against you. Most importantly, you have seen God working in your life. The gestalt that is you has been considered and reflected on.

In attempting to determine your future life path, your foundation will rest on serving God with what He has given you, the critical junctions He sends into your life, and accepting the responsibilities God has given you. You are the steward of your life, and you must do it well.

Ephesians 5:17 tells us, "Therefore do not be foolish, but understand what the Lord's will is." The more you try to understand His will, the more God will be able to help you.

The Wrong Path

Distressingly, we may determine that our current path is not His choice for us. We may become painfully aware that we are going down the wrong path when we consider Christianity as our way of life. So how do we know we are going down the wrong path? Clues can be our frustration with our lives, short tempers, a general confusion, depression,

195

anxiety, etc. You might find yourself like that Energizer bunny that keeps pounding and pounding that same drum over and over until you, and possibly everyone around you, are ready to march to the beat of a different drummer. At the point of exhaustion, we finally realize we cannot kill that bunny with a wooden stake and silver bullets and are ready to bail out into a different life.

The movie *All That Jazz* showed the protagonist starting each day looking in the mirror and saying, "It's showtime folks." His life was just a show to him. We may realize we are going down the wrong path when we start seeing our life as something of a show. We step into life each morning playing a role we are not well suited for, but don't know what else to do.

We may discover that our fear of change is the biggest obstacle to the changes we need. We would rather live with the seven dragons we know than the one we don't know. Change is hard and often painful, but it is often the cost of growth. We can make changes and grow as we accept, embrace, and follow His path for us. As noted, the Bible talks about those who are satisfied with their lives and live it without concern as they follow His path for them. Ecclesiastes 5:18-20 states, "This is what I have observed to be good: that it is appropriate for a person to eat, to drink, and to find satisfaction in their toilsome labor under the sun during the few days of life God has given them – for this is their lot. Moreover, when God gives someone wealth and possessions, and the ability to enjoy them, to accept their lot and be happy in their toil – this is a gift of God. They seldom reflect on the days of their life, because God keeps them occupied with gladness of heart."

If you finally conclude that you are on the wrong path, you can lean on C.S. Lewis for support, "You can't go back and change the beginning, but you can start where you are and change the ending."

The Bible

God has decided that you and I will go through certain things in our lives, be certain types of people, and live certain types of lives. Whether we actively include Him in our lives will be our decision, but to include Him, we must read His Bible. This is indispensable.

As mentioned in the Foundation Puzzle Pieces chapter, there is a common core set of beliefs central to all Christians, including the Bible being God's sacred, infallible word. There are many additional and sometimes conflicting beliefs between denominations, but know that God's path for you will be within the core beliefs. From there, He may guide you to a denomination He knows would be best for you to serve Him.

The words we read will be the same for all of us, but how the Bible impacts our lives can be very individualistic. Our current life problems may be duly addressed as we read our Bible, or they may never seem spoken of. Sections may seem specifically written for us, or the words may seem confusing. Understanding may be proportional to the effort we put into trying to understand His words to us. Understanding may be granted us as we grow in faith. Sometimes we need to build a foundation of Biblical knowledge by not only reading our Bible, but other books that assist in Christian growth. Writings by Rick Warren, Charles Spurgeon, and C.S. Lewis have served me in that regard.

When I decided to write a book based on Jeremiah 29:11, I knew I needed to first reread Matthew, Mark, Luke, John, Proverbs, and Ecclesiastes prior to reading Jeremiah. A refresher of the Gospels was a necessary foundation. Proverbs and Ecclesiastes followed in an attempt to glean some of their wisdom. Only then did I feel ready to read Jeremiah and write this book.

Our understanding of Biblical truths, the profound meanings we discover, and the directions the Bible provides can be a life-long source of personal inspiration and guidance for the life we are being called to lead.

He will place people, circumstances, and trials before us. He will send us disappointments, surprises, hopes, and a future. When we face them, we can drink deeply from the Bible's fountain of knowledge, or, as noted earlier, we can gargle a bit and spit it out. Many have done both, but in all cases, it was left up to the individual to choose.

Feeding Your Future

Once you have assembled your Life Puzzle pieces as best you can, once you have determined your path in life as best as you are able, once you have made Christianity your way of life, you will need to feed your future. It can be fed or it can be starved. God leaves this to you to decide upon.

A minister in my church told the story of an American Indian who was telling the youth of his tribe how we have two wolves inside us. One is ravenous and filled with anger, pain, and pride. The other is ravenous and filled with peace, serenity, and joy. They are in a fight to the death. When one of the youth asked who will win, he replied, "The one you feed."

You will feed your wolf through the way you lead your life, through how you treat your fellow man, through your use of your self-will, and through how well you follow Christ.

Assembling Your Puzzle

It is now time to put your many Life Puzzle pieces together. It is now time to incorporate the many facets you have uncovered into a Self-Definition of the unique you that God loves so dearly, develop a coherent Mission Statement on what your future could entail, and create a Plan of Action on how you will live out your Christ-centered life. You will attempt to articulate His plan for you, well aware that it will evolve throughout your life as he calls upon you to fulfill the destiny He specifically designed for you.

Start by reviewing your previous chapter's puzzle piece questions and answers. Do not be surprised if you adjust some of your answers or see the meanings of them differently now that you look at them in retrospect. Note any findings, priorities, and responsibilities that seem significant. This review will serve as a grounding in what you currently are.

Next, you will write three essays. Each should be no more than a page in length. Ambiguous, uncertain, and tentative phrasing will be normal and expected given we are the ambiguous, uncertain, and tentative human race. Simply make a serious moral effort and trust in God while understanding that there will be things you will not understand today, but may tomorrow.

Proverbs 3:5-6 tells us, "Trust in the Lord with all your heart and lean not on your understanding; in all your ways submit to Him, and He will make your paths straight."

Immediately before you start to write these three essays, place things in perspective by reflecting on Hebrews 12:1-3, "Therefore, since we are surrounded by such a great cloud of witnesses, let us throw off everything that hinders and the sin that so easily entangles. And let us run with perseverance the race marked out for us, fixing our eyes on Jesus, the pioneer and perfecter of faith. For the joy set before him he endured the cross, scorning its shame, and sat down at the right hand of the throne of God. Consider him who endured such opposition from sinners, so that you will not grow weary and lose heart."

Run with purpose. Run with determination. Run with exhilaration. Throw off all that hinders the life that God Himself wants for you.

Self-Definition

Complete a self-definition by answering the following, "From what puzzle pieces I have learned about myself and what God has shown me, I define myself as:"

Mission Statement

Complete a mission statement by answering the following, "As best I am able to understand God's unique and loving plan for me and what the puzzle pieces of my life seem to indicate, I feel the life path I am being called upon to serve Him contains:"

Plan of Action

Complete a plan of action by answering the following, "As best as I am able to understand God's life plan for me from both puzzle pieces and the empty areas of the puzzle, I will attempt to live Christianity as my way of life by:"

Conclusion

As the beloved of the Lord, you have written something of the story of your life. This started and ended in the pause you took to read and work through this book. Some chapters of your life may seem weak and some strong. Some paths you have trod are short, some long, some barely lasted one day, and some are always here to stay. But now it is time to live the prosperity, hope, and a future promised you in Jeremiah 29:11.

"'For I know the plans I have for you,' declares the Lord, 'plans to prosper you and not to harm you, plans to give you hope and a future.'"

17. References

Avshalom Caspi, e. a. (2003). Children's Behavioral Styles at Age 3 are Linked to their Adult personality traits at age 26. *Journal of Personality, 71(4)*, 496-513.

Avshalom Caspi, e. a. (2003). *Children's Behavioral Styles at Age 3 are Linked to their Adult personality traits at age 26.* Retrieved from http://education-consumers.org/issues-public-education-reseach -analysis/childrens-behavioral-styles/: http://education-consumers.org/issues-public-education-reseach -analysis/childrens-behavioral-styles/

Bitette, N. (2016, January 12). *Curse of the lottery: Tragic stories of big jackpot winners.* Retrieved from http://www.nydailynews.com: http://www.nydailynews.com/life-style/tragic-stories-lottery-winners-article-1.2492941

Corporation for National & Community Service. (2015). *Quick Facts*. Retrieved from Volunteering and Civic Life in America 2015: http://www.volunteeringinamerica.gov

Fowler, B. F. (1975). *Benton & Fowler's Best, Worst, and Most Unusual.* Greenwich, CT: Information House Books, Inc.

Friendship. (n.d.). Retrieved from Wikipedia.org: https://en.m.wikipedia.org/wiki/Friendship

Johnson, D. R. (2010, August 6). *Our-Personality-Is-Fully-Developed-By-the-Age-of-7-151093*. Retrieved from http://news.softpedia.com/news/Our-Personality-Is-Fully-Developed-By-the-Age-of-7-151093.shtm:

http://news.softpedia.com/news/Our-Personality-Is-Fully-Developed-By-the-Age-of-7-151093.shtm

List of dreams. (2016, February 6). Retrieved from Wikipedia: https://en.wikipedia.org/wiki/List_of_dreams

Lvcifer. (2011, February 16). *The Entire Case History of Robbie Mannheim: The Real-Life Story That Inspired "The Exorcist" Movie.* Retrieved from Diabolicalconfusions: https://diabolicalconfusions.wordpress.com/2011/02/16/the-story-of-r-the-real-life-story-that-inspired-the-exorcist/

Maldonado, J. (n.d.). *6 Lessons To Teach Your Children About Money.* Retrieved from Searcy Finanical web site: http://www.searcyfinancial.com/blog-posts/84-planning-for-the-family/7-6-lessons-to-teach-your-children-about-money

McKeever, B. (2019, January 3). *The Nonprofit Sector in Brief.* Retrieved from https://nccs.urban.org/project/nonprofit-sector-brief

Passell, P. (1977). *The Best Encore.* New York: Ballantine Books.

Peck, M. S. (1983). *People of the Lie: The Hope for Healing Human Evil.* New York, NY: Simon & Schuster, Inc.

Peter, L. J. (1977). *Peter's Quotations.* New York: William Morrow and Company, Inc.

Quick Facts About Nonprofits. (2015, December). Retrieved from http://nccs.urban.org/: http://nccs.urban.org/statistics/quickfacts.cfm

Sias, P. M., & Bartoo, H. (2007). Low-cost approaches to promote physical and mental health: Theory, research, and practice. In P. M. Sias, & H. Bartoo, *Low-cost approaches to promote physical and mental health* (pp. 455-475). New York: Springer New York.

Tomlinson, S. (2013, October 8). *The Devil in Roland Doe: How the 1973 horror film The Exorcist was based on a real-life possession in Missouri.* Retrieved from http://www.dailmail.co.uk/news/article-2449423/Devil-

Roland-Doe-The-Exorcist-based-real-life-Missouri-possession.html: http://www.dailmail.co.uk/news/article-2449423/Devil-Roland-Doe-The-Exorcist-based-real-life-Missouri-possession.html

Made in the USA
Coppell, TX
25 July 2025

52329312R00115